MOB RULE

Lessons Learned by a Mother of Boys

Hannah Evans

B L O O M S B U R Y

LONDON · NEW DELHI · NEW YORK · SYDNEY

First published in Great Britain 2013

Copyright © 2013 by Hannah Evans

The moral right of the author has been asserted

Bloomsbury Publishing, London, New Delhi, New York and Sydney

50 Bedford Square, London WC1B 3DP

A CIP catalogue record for this book is available from the British Library

ISBN 978 1 4088 3012 3
10 9 8 7 6 5 4 3 2 1

Typeset by Hewer Text UK Ltd, Edinburgh

Printed in Great Britain by CPI Group (UK) Ltd, Croydon CR0 4YY

www.bloomsbury.com/hannahevans

For Charles, Toby, Barney and Josh . . . my boys – big
and small – without whom life wouldn't be nearly
as noisy or half as much fun.

mob n. female of the species who breeds male member(s) of society; mother of boy(s).

Warning:

This book contains gratuitous stereotypes
and gross generalisations.

Contents

The Cast

The MOB

The Mother of Boys. Always exhausted, often exasperated, but nevertheless totally enamoured with her trio of testosterone and biggest boy husband. Most commonly spotted in jeans and a fleece. Very occasionally seen sporting a skirt.

The FOB

The Father of Boys. Darling dad to his litter of lads, long-suffering husband to the merciless MOB. Often away due to Naval career, but still entirely – make that *overly* – in tune with his all-male offspring.

Sensible Son

Firstborn king of the castle. Reflective, straight-talking and old beyond his years. A slightly smaller carbon copy of the towering FOB. Deaf to the world when in front of a screen.

Binary Boy

Number-two contender for the throne. A hot head of energy and copious cuddles, he's either switched 'On' and unbeatable or 'Off' and insufferable. Fortunately, increasingly more 'On' than 'Off'. Never happier than when outside and messing in mud.

Feisty Fellow

Number-three court-jester son. Born running and trying to catch up with, or overtake, his siblings ever since. Always smiling, rarely stationary. Still impatiently waiting for his gorgeous 'girl curls' to be cut.

The GOBs

The adored and adoring Grandparents of Boys. Only those with energy and enthusiasm should consider playing this part. Although the ability to explain algebra will stand you in good stead.

The MOG

The Mother of Girls. Smiles at the MOB sympathetically, sanctimoniously or possibly not at all. May huddle her girls off in the opposite direction or encourage them to muck in with your gaggle of guys.

Manicured MOG

That Mother of Girls who *always* looks great. You know . . . *her*.

Manicured MOB

Apparently exists, but a *much* scarcer species.

Kindred MOB

A firm, but fair, Mother of Boys. Accepts the age-old adage of 'boys will be boys' – within limits. Hers. Knows very well what a 'fizzy willy' is, but refuses to drive faster just to bring one about.

Extreme MOB

The original Mother of manic, mad Boys. Apparently, happily oblivious to the dangers of, and damage caused by, her swash-buckling sons. Possibly short-sighted, probably hard of hearing.

Perfect Pair

The balanced combination of the MOB and the MOG. Often feted by society, she is quick to remind you that even on her purportedly 'perfect' planet, her 'spice' and 'snail' offspring aren't always sweetness and light.

Gorgeous Girl

The antidote to khaki.

Prologue

The church is warm and welcoming. Wooden pews stuffed to the brim with snug winter coats and stripy scarves. The organ wheezes to a halt and the vicar peers, owl-expectantly, out and over his bifocals. Both his and the seasonally expansive congregation's breath are bated.

Gorgeous Girl skips to the front, faces her audience. Smoothes her piece of paper, opens her mouth. 'The reading today is tak—'

She stops abruptly, turns her head, frowns. To my left, I see her dad smiling at her, encouragingly. She gulps a little, and tries again.

I see her mum smiling too, but she has followed her daughter's frown. I, in turn, smile and also follow her frown. I look towards the children's corner, where a glory of girls sit, heads bent low, tongues lodged firmly in the corners of mouths, diligently colouring in sparkling angels. And where . . .

Gorgeous Girl reads on.

I shiver despite the warmth, as I scan our pew. Sensible Son is there, head inclined and hymn sheet in hand. Binary Boy is there – jiggling his 'Can't-you-*ever*-sit-still?' behind, granted, but there none the less. The FOB is there, tall and dark and staring man-happy into space. So that just leaves . . .

'Feisty Fellow . . . where's Feisty Fellow?' I hiss at my husband. 'I thought he was sitting on your lap!'

'He was,' the FOB hisses back, 'but he wanted to go and play with his friend.'

'And you *let* him?' I squeal, earning myself a silencing stare from the row in front. The FOB shrugs. With an increasing sense of female foreboding, I crane my neck round a large stone pillar to try to locate our smallest son. No need.

Without warning, Feisty Fellow explodes into view and crashes to a halt in front of the pulpit. Best Boy Friend follows, hot and sweaty on his heels, aiming a Stickle Brick bazooka at Feisty Fellow's back. They pant.

'Don't shoot . . .' yells Feisty Fellow, exhibiting an astonishing understanding of the power of acoustics. Best Boy Friend stands firm, legs apart, firearm fixed. He repositions his weapon and begins to utter increasingly loud machine-gun stutters.

'Don't . . . don't shoot *me*, or . . .' – Feisty Fellow brandishes the rag doll he's been hitherto holding captive against his chest – 'Baby Jeshush!'

A none-too-holy hush descends on the church.

Someone titters from the direction of the font.

'Oh Lord,' I mutter, mainly to myself, but you never know.

'Quite!' agrees Silent Stare from in front.

'Do carry on, dear,' says the vicar helpfully to Gorgeous Girl. Valiantly, she ploughs on.

Face burning brighter than a Christmas pud, I excuse my way apologetically along the length of the pew and direct my trainee terrorist less than delicately towards the door. As we stumble outside into the frozen night, Gorgeous Girl finally finishes her reading.

'Amen,' she says, with the slightest of sighs.

'*A* men to that,' I echo, '*A* bloomin' men.' I tuck Feisty Fellow under one arm and we hurry on home.

LESSON 1:

Joining the MOB

I haven't always been a MOB.

Once upon a time, I was an ordinary woman with a pretty ordinary husband and, together, we led an (almost) ordinary life. He went to sea, I went to work and at weekends, sometimes, we went to Ikea. We laughed at *Friends*, we cried at the airport, we took it in turns to empty the dishwasher and bins. We conformed pretty much to the married norm.

Then just as things were tocking away nicely, my biological clock began to tick. Fast, furious and increasingly loud. It kept me awake at night, it buzzed in my head all day. Only now, after the hours and the years of my Duracell darlings, am I able to appreciate the irony of this 24/7 stimulus.

Luckily for me and my reproductive Rolex, my other half's time piece was synchronised with my own, and so – in the time it takes you to realise in Sainsbury's that having a baby's not necessarily the best thing since that sliced bread you've forgotten because you're too busy dealing with a screaming bundle of snot – we found ourselves ecstatically, excitedly and, somewhat scarily, 'with child'.

Over celebratory Shloer and what felt like overnight, I would morph from an invisible working woman to a majestic mother-in-waiting. Suddenly, I'd see pushchairs and prams where I'd swear there'd been none, I'd clock babies and bumps that I'd previously passed by, buy magazines and manuals that I'd previously decried. No longer just anyone, I would now be pregnant with a capital 'P': expecting to be adored, adoring expecting and accepting – graciously – each and every seat I'd be sure to be given.

Or rather, I would've done all of the above, as I've been assured by my fecund friends that *they* did, had I not spent the entire first trimester and, come to think of it, most of the second, prone, at home and within vomiting distance of a lavatory.

'It says here that morning sickness normally eases at around three months . . .' says the Future Father helpfully, scanning the 'sick' section of one of my recently acquired manuals of motherhood. 'But you're *way* past that, aren't you? According to this, you should be "blooming" by now!'

I raise my retching head with as much dignity as I can muster and fix my husband with a McEnroe glare.

'I'm so . . . sorry . . . not to . . . be . . . normal!' I chunder, before renewing my acquaintance with the bottom of the loo.

'Oh well, we can't all do everything by the book, can we?' he says cheerfully, putting down the manual and holding back my hair.

Apparently in reprieve, I gulp back any outraged expletives and reach instead for a ginger cookie. Let's hope that there's more to *this* manual myth than the twelve-week nausea fallacy, I think wryly, before stuffing the allegedly stomach-calming biscuit into my 'blooming' mouth.

At eighteen weeks, my husband and I are visited by our midwife.

Apologising profusely for her permanently cold hands (surely a propensity for Raynaud's should automatically exclude you from a career in midwifery?), she slathers my ever-tauter tummy with equally frigid and unnecessarily large amounts of what looks – and feels – like frog spawn. It drips down the steep slopes of my stomach and on to the sofa on which I lie, beached.

I resist the urge to wipe it off and wait expectantly.

With one deft move, she skates the stethoscope over my body before skidding – suddenly – to a stop.

A thundering, rhythmic beat booms out from the Doppler box and the Future Father and I listen, entranced, in awe, to our very own baby's in-utero heart.

After a minute or two, the midwife breaks our spellbound silence.

'Ahhh,' she says and smiles. 'A full-on, fast heartbeat. A girl, I'd say . . . most definitely a girl.'

Despite her glacial fingers and the sub-zero spawn, a deep, warm glow envelops my body.

A girl. Of course. It makes perfect sense to me. Yes, I am a woman. And I will be having . . . a girl.

In my day, after thirty weeks you had to get a doctor's note if you wanted to fly. After thirty weeks, I reflect grumpily, I won't be able to fit through the door of the plane, let alone be, in any way, shape or form fit to actually go anywhere. With enormous difficulty and a great deal of prima-madonna puffing, I eventually manage to clamp the seatbelt shut over my protesting twenty-eight week protrusion and circle my already swollen ankles in preparation for take-off. The Future Father squeezes my hand, and as the plane soars skywards, I allow my eyes to flutter shut.

Eight uncomfortable hours and a mere forty-seven trips to the toilet later, we touch down, and I lumber out for our precious pre-baby break on the Caribbean island of sunny St Lucia.

We make the most of our final freedom. Together, we take ancient buses blaring Marley to secluded pieces of sparkling paradise. As one, we laze, read and doze under flickering palms, woken, occasionally, by the thumping rhythm of distant drums. Hand in unhurried hand, we stroll through the hustling markets of tiny towns, bingeing on bananas, coconuts and fish.

The St Lucians are ultra-attentive, extra-forthcoming, especially, it seems, towards a woman in my all too apparent 'condition'. Our path is blocked by a larger-than-life character and we stop to pass the time of day.

'You's all out front, Mumma,' grins my new best St Lucian ladyfriend, rubbing my belly enthusiastically. My stomach shifts sideways, aiming a well-practised heel kick in her general direction. I force an uncomfortable smile, trying to put aside my very British reservations about being manhandled by a complete stranger – albeit a very friendly one – in the middle of Soufrière High Street.

'You's got a little g'rrl cookin' in der, I'm tinkin',' she prophesies with biblical conviction, before ambling onwards.

'What a load of unscientific rubbish!' I chuckle out loud. Nevertheless, I think, placing a proprietary hand over the expanse of my bump, it's more grist to the growing girl mill.

Unlike my laconic ladyfriend however, I keep my musings to myself.

Three months later.

'I . . . really . . . think . . . we . . . should've . . . left . . . for the hospital sooner!'

The Future Father takes his eyes momentarily off the road to study the butt that almost entirely obscures his rear-view mirror. Unable to lower myself into the bucket front seat of our Renault Scenic, I have positioned myself – doggy style – in the back of the car, from whence I gaze drunkenly and somewhat nauseously at the unsuspecting drivers of vehicles behind.

'What did you say, my love?' he asks tenderly.

'I (huff) said (argggh) – oh, never mind. Can you (oooh) hurry up now?'

'Will do,' he replies, putting foot to the floor.

6

'Owwww . . . not so fast! Slow (huffing) down, will you?' I scream perfectly reasonably at my confused.com.

My innocent other half has yet to realise that whatever he does for this hormonal mother-to-be over the next twelve hours – or indeed, twelve years – will be, quite frankly, wrong.

He soon will.

Ten hours and forty-three minutes later.

Astonished blue, almost black eyes stare up at me from the swilling waters of the once pristine pool. Startled, I stare back. With the absolute concentration of an unaccustomed drunk, I take my naked newborn into my arms, petrified of hurting the too-long limbs, of insufficiently cradling the blotchy, bald head. Hungrily, I fold slippery skin against my own and watch in intoxicated awe as the concave chest rises and falls. Rises . . . and falls.

A mother – me? Yes, I shudder, I am a *mother*.

I gaze at my infant, still semi-detached. I take in the cord – pulsating; the mottled curve of my baby's belly; onwards . . . and down.

And at that moment I see. It. The Willy. HE.

Standing to attention, demanding attention. Bold, as they say, as brass. And with 'it' comes an unexpected realisation. Yes, I have become a mother. But more specifically – and just a touch terrifyingly, I, me, SHE, have become the Mother of . . . a *Boy*. Over what feels like an eternity, but what is actually overnight, I have become . . . a MOB.

It's a Tuesday evening very like any other, eight months on. My sporadically domesticated husband is ironing his work shirts. I don't do work shirts and he can iron a crease as sharp as any of my sleep-deprived digs, so, for once, I concede to his superior

Serviceman skills. Anyway, tonight I have other female fish to fry. Unobserved, I grab my bag and skedaddle to the loo.

Two minutes later I'm back by his side.

'Oh,' I say inadequately, as I thrust the plastic stick in front of the all-too-freshly Father of Boy's face. The plastic stick, entirely innocuous only moments before, is now sporting not one, but two, prophetically blue lines. 'Oh,' I repeat.

With customary calm, the FOB puts the iron carefully down, blanches ever so slightly and hugs me . . . tight. And then we begin to giggle, uncontrollably, manically, verging on hysterically. Upstairs, our barely more than infant Sensible Son, supposedly sound asleep, lets out an indignant wail through the floorboards. I extricate myself from my other half's arms and sprint to his side.

'Make the most of this, wee man,' I croon as I cradle my first-born decadently in my arms. 'Cos you're not going to be the only king in this castle for much longer!'

Seven months later, the contender to number-one son's throne shoots on to the stage, both his amniotic sac and lungs all too obviously intact.

'They say it's lucky for a baby to be born without the membranes breaking,' my Oldest (and child-free) Friend informs me, placing an extra-large box of chocolates on the bedside trolley and eyeing me and my offspring with dubious concern.

Sensible Son, ecstatic that he can once again sit right on top of me, rather than perching precariously on the edge of my bump, is more excited by the arrival of the chocolates than of his Binary Boy brother. Clinging to the bed frame, he reaches over to help himself, sending both truffles and trolley scooting into the next-door cubicle and narrowly missing an incoming nurse.

'Are you going to be OK?' asks said friend, restraining the

fifteen-month-old with one hand and stroking the newborn's downy cheek with the other.

'We'll be fine, won't we, my boys?' I sing.

The G&T jollity of gas and air obviously takes some time to subside.

According to the dates, my husband is at sea when we conceive our third child. But while his uniform is immaculate, the conception is presumably not, and so I am forced to admit that even if our practicals appear to be perfect, the data may be dodgy. Science will never be my strongest suit.

We take our boys along to the twenty-week scan.

'My, you've got your hands full!' comments the enviously toned, implausibly young and exceptionally insightful sonographer, slapping on the spawn and rolling her scanner over my reinflated bulge.

Too exhausted to respond to her oh-so-candid comment, I allow myself instead to wallow in the wonder of a rare horizontal moment. My battered body, I reflect with a mixture of exasperation and pride, has become more adept than the government at coping with inflationary pressures on a regular basis. What 'back to normal' looks like, I have no idea.

'Yes, there he is . . . looks like everything's fine. We'll just take some measurements . . .'

'He?' I croak, straining every one of my abdominals to hoist my head from the pillow. 'You said, "he"?'

'Did I? Sorry. I always say "he". Did you want to know the sex of this little one?'

The FOB and I look at each other; nod. Unlike our slightly earlier-than-planned pregnancy, we've discussed this – at length – over baby-filled days and broken nights.

We hadn't wanted to find out for Sensible Son or Binary

Boy. Hadn't wanted to furtively shake our presents and spoil the surprise of what was inside. But this time is different. This time, I don't feel the need for any more surprises: like the burgeoning Boy Scout I am destined to become, I'd really rather 'Be prepared'.

Because whatever the answer, I want to know sooner when I am marginally more sane, rather than later, when I will undoubtedly, be significantly more sore. Because I want to deal with any emotional fallout, while my insides haven't. Because I know, deep down in the depths of my girl-getting mind, that I don't want to run the risk of feeling even the tiniest bit deflated, when everything, and everyone, says I should be elated. So I need to know, and I need to know – now.

For weeks before my fourth birthday, I begged my parents for a Tiny Tears. I coveted that chubby doll that cried 'real' tears from her plastic eyes and peed 'real' wee from a pin-prick hole below her bulging belly. I wanted to cradle her, dress her in tunics, stroke her platinum, polyester hair. I would make her beautiful, parade her proudly in her pint-size pram and sing her to sleep with my own childhood songs. I would love her more than I loved life itself, and I would call my baby 'Katy'.

When I was six, I cast Katy aside. Katy was out because Sindy was in. Sindy, with the ridiculously long legs, impossibly luscious locks and a stripy yellow and orange tracksuit, topped off, a little alarmingly, with rubber red stilettos. In my 'house' under my built-in bed, and in the absence of confiding sisters, Sindy and I rapidly became bosom buddies. We talked about horses, about today's best friend (albeit a different one from yesterday's) about my thoroughly exasperating and fem-alien Big Brother. He was not in the slightest bit interested in Sindy. Nor, thankfully, was she interested in him. Sindy was all mine.

Sindy's reign didn't last long. Because just before I turned seven, silicone Sindy was replaced – brusquely and bitchily – by real-life Rebecca. Real-life Rebecca was my Scandinavian baby cousin – round-eyed and ruddy-cheeked – and that summer she needed real-life looking after. By me.

Willingly, I spooned mountains of mush into her open mouth, moronically aping her every facial move. Deliriously, I tickled her tummy, eliciting attacks of the most glorious of giggles. In seventh heaven, I even tackled her most nauseous of nappies, relishing – yes, relishing – the opportunity to put years of plastic play into actual practice. Rebecca didn't seem to sleep much during the day that holiday. Her over-zealous, but well-meaning, surrogate 'mum' cousin made *very* sure of that.

And so those minutes, hours, days of Katy, Sindy and Rebecca, of dressing and undressing, of ponytails and pretty princesses have prepared me, conditioned me, made me aspire to being the Mother of a Girl, just once upon a time in my now boy-bound life.

I want to see what a chick off the old block looks like, sounds like, *is* like, rather than my thus far entirely male masonry. Want to clasp my daughter's hand as my mother did mine, to curse inappropriate boyfriends behind her back, to glow with maternal pride at my imaginary girl, the blushing bride.

Let's face it, I want to buy the stripy tights and patterned pinafores. Hell, I want to really *need* a hairbrush.

And, instead, here I am, almost thirty years after Rebecca's reign, with the odds fairly precariously stacked against me. Two boys in two years, with number three simmering away nicely. The chances of our overactive third being of the female variety are, according to both folklore and fact (and unlike my mid-trimester self), extremely slim.

The sonographer wields her weapon of mass deduction. 'Yup,

there we go, Mrs Evans, there's no mistaking this one . . . it's a little boy.'

I swallow hard, smile up at the FOB through blurry eyes. Grasp my sons' sweaty hands in mine.

'Look guys,' I choke, 'we're having a baby boy!'

'Anovva' bruvva?' asks our two-year-old overthrown king of the castle, gazing first at my stomach and then at the screen.

I wipe my eyes and smile broadly. 'Yes, my boys. Anovva' bruvva.'

That's it then. Officially and irrevocably. No Tiny Tears, no tights, no princesses, no pink. I am joining the ranks of the multiple MOB.

Feisty Fellow plops into existence with astonishing alacrity. One minute I'm eating chips in the hospital canteen, the next I'm fishing both them and my baby out of the birthing pool. I haven't been able to go near French Fries since. There are obviously upsides to childbirth, after all.

Feisty Fellow is big, blond and all-over beautiful; his parents are immediately and utterly besotted.

Up, about and out within twenty-four hours of his birth, the now fully fledged FOB and I take our gang for celebratory scampi at a local pub. We settle ourselves into a covert corner. Sensible Son and Binary Boy build ketchup-sachet structures, while Feisty Fellow plugs in for a feed. The waitress approaches our tableau of testosterone.

'Oooh, look,' she squeals, 'what an adorable family!' I flush with post-natal hormones and maternal pride. 'And a teeny tiny baby. How old is she?'

I smooth the spun silk hair from Feisty Fellow's forehead. 'She is a "he" actually,' I correct softly.

'Oooh, er . . . sorry. I didn't realise. Oh, well, never mind!' she squeaks, a smidgen less enthusiastically.

'Never mind?' I repeat, raising my eyebrows and glancing protectively at my mercifully oblivious older offspring.

'Oh, I . . . er . . . I meant . . .' She tries in vain to cover her tactless tracks. 'Anyway, you've still got time to go for a girl!'

If my eyebrows could go higher they'd leap off my head.

'Anyway . . .' It's her turn to flush. 'Right – well, what can I get you?'

I give her the full force of my post-partum glare. 'I don't suppose there's humble pie on the menu?' I say sweetly. 'Failing that, I'll have scampi. No chips.'

She nods, smiles weakly and scuttles to the kitchen.

Let that be a lesson to you, I think, kissing my sons, one by blessed one.

It's never a good idea to mess with the MOB.

You know you've joined the MOB
when you hear . . .

- 'My, are they all yours?'
- 'How fantastic . . . halfway to a football team!' (Generally from a man)
- 'Cheer up, it took me four tries to get *my* girl.' (Mostly from a woman)
- 'Bless you!' (Occasionally)
- 'Poor you!' (Frequently)
- 'Lucky you!' (Once)
- 'How *do* you cope?'
- 'You've got your hands full!'
- And of course, the ultimate: 'So . . . are you going for a girl?'

Wanted: Female Wonder Woman to be a 'Mother of Boys'

Our client is looking for a full-time carer to take overall ownership and responsibility for three bouncy boys under four and their in-and-out FOB.

The ideal candidate can make mountains of stew out of molehills of meat, is able to answer a barrage of boy queries beginning with 'Why' and will have an appropriately accommodating sense of smell. Heavy housework a distinct possibility. Experience of herding sheep and shift work a bonus. Experience of hairdressing: entirely unnecessary. GSOH is non-negotiable. Must be available 24/7 and able to start . . . er, yesterday.

Salary: cold coffees in Costa and a new pair of jeans (lifetime guarantee).

Only serious applicants are invited to apply.
Only serious applicants won't have the time.

Hush a boy baby

There is, I believe, a lot to be said for the idea of living life backwards.

If you did, you'd take numerous photos of your teenage tummy and post them on your Facebook home page, instead of hiding your paltry puppy fat under your father's extra-large sweater.

If you did, you'd thank your mother for sequestrating that lollipop from your party bag before you could get your mitts within tooth-rotting distance of its globby, grey stick.

And if you did, you'd haul yourself and your burgeoning bump off the sofa and drag it to the cinema while you could still squish your butt into one seat not two, could choose something other than an animated U and didn't have to cash in your kids' ISAs for both a cinema ticket *and* a boil-ridden babysitter.

Actually, scrub all the above. If I could've lived life backwards, I would've spent the vast majority of my pre-boy years in preparation. In bed. Asleep.

Hindsight is indeed a wonderful thing.

For our sons, bless their snugly socks, are good at very many things. But, unfortunately for both the FOB and me (although I feel it is my duty to point out that hot-bunking in a submarine appears to be the perfect training for remaining entirely oblivious to the nocturnal wails of a child), sleep is most definitely not one of them.

You could be forgiven, therefore, for wondering what on earth possessed us to add to our stable of sons with such startling speed. On the other hand, you might surmise (correctly) that the total absence of rational thought engendered by perpetual sleep deprivation is the ideal state in which to add – rapidly – to an already insomniac, and quite probably insane, family.

I personally have never been able to keep my eyes open long enough to ponder the issue at length.

Our family sleep saga started out auspiciously enough.

When I was pregnant with Sensible Son, I worked from home. And being a 'virgin' mother-to-be, I was, of course, the most uncomfortable, most needy and undoubtedly most exhausted person on this planet.

'Put your feet up!' counselled those in the know. 'You've got to look after yourself and the baby – take it easy.' And so I did.

Taking full advantage of my short commute from kitchen to study, I'd roll out of bed at something after eight, before pottering downstairs for a quiet cup of tea. After lunch, I'd burrow back under my sometimes still-warm duvet and catch forty (if not fifty) winks. And then, when it got dark, I'd have a long, lingering bath, pull on my accommodating pyjamas and sink, spent, on to the sofa to catch the latest mugging or murder from Albert Square. My unwittingly selfish pre-baby world according to . . . me.

On the odd night, before my eyelids and exhaustion got the better of me, I might even manage to imbibe a few moments of 'A Manual'.

I like manuals. From the Pony Club guide to buffing your bridle, to 100 Student Strategies for surviving on a pittance, I have, for as long as I can remember (which admittedly these days rarely extends beyond about teatime yesterday), been a great fan of learning from the experiences – good and bad – of others. It appeals, I suppose, to my sense of order, of control, that there is a right way and a wrong way of doing things, that $a + b = c$, that as long as I follow the recipe religiously, there is a good chance that my Victoria sponge will spring effortlessly from its tin, flavoursome and fluffy.

It has taken me some not insignificant time to realise that, unlike my cakes, my offspring do not always rise, as expected and as predicted, on every occasion.

Way back when, however, in the days 'Before Boy', I was under the delusion that information was everything, and so I read. I devoured the manuals, the books, the hand-me-down bibles of generations of mothers, each tome oozing abundant amounts of often conflicting advice, of dos and do nots, of must haves and should nots, until my brain felt almost – but never quite – as bulging as my bump.

And then, armed with a wealth of wisdom and with my chosen routine at my swollen fingertips, I embarked on an approach to motherhood that would, I felt sure, transport me from ignorant innocent to model mum. If my enthusiastically informed imagination (not to mention pages 23–40) were anything to go by, my clockwork cupcake would, within weeks, be gurgling happily beside his sleep-satiated parent as she bumbled round the kitchen making jellies and jam.

The bun in my oven, however, had other ideas.

For the first ten days of his life, my guinea-pig poppet does indeed behave immaculately, lulling me and my nearest and dearest into a distinctly false and decidedly fragile sense of security. He wakes, he cries, he eats, he sleeps. He does very little else. I plug my newborn in and he, it appears, obediently and according to plan, passes out. I coo, he's content. Everyone's happy.

On day eleven, however, it all goes horribly wrong.

I am on to my third slice of toast and honey (I realise that strictly speaking it should be one and a half, but hey, this eating

21

for two's a hungry habit to kick) when Sensible Son, uncharacteristically and unbidden, *wakes up*.

I stare at the kitchen clock: 07:48. Isn't he still supposed to be asleep, blissfully blacked out in his nocturnal nest? I consult my manual. Yes, here we go. Page 30, paragraph 3, subsection C. My memory has not (surprisingly) failed me. He is indeed supposed to be sound asleep, and yet here he is, emphatically awake . . . and wailing down the airwaves for all the world (or at least our near neighbours) to hear. What on earth has gone wrong?

I creep upstairs, hoping, praying that he will somehow have 'settled himself' back to sleep by the time I peep surreptitiously into his Moses basket. To my horror, he has not. And even I, a total learner in the art of kid communication, can see that while sleep may be very much on my agenda, it is, most blatantly, not on his. What now? In theory, I should leave him to it, let him cry. But . . .

Aware that I might be forever blotting my contented copybook, I pick up my bawling child and rock him gently, sssshing and shushing until his sobbing subsides and my outraged infant closes his eyes. Drinking in the silence with rookie relief, I lower my now dormant son back into his cot before tiptoeing, with the stealth, if not quite the figure, of a cat burglar, towards the door.

Waaaaahhhh.

'Shhh,' I soothe hopefully from the hall. 'Shhhh . . .'

To no avail. Three aborted attempts at escape later, I finally give in to my uninstructed instincts and offered him a bulging boob. The clock reads 07:54; my disobedient son is six minutes early.

At five months, he continues to misbehave.

He should, apparently, be sleeping soundly through the night, allowing his milking-machine mother an uninterrupted eight hours of sanity-inducing sleep. My bouncing boy, however, can barely manage four before waking me vociferously for yet another starlit snack.

'It's the sign of an intelligent baby . . . an active mind,' says one ever-buoyant friend, studiously ignoring my increasingly frazzled face. I stare at her through bleary kohl eyes and make a mental note to remove the brain-training mobile from above his cot the minute she leaves. Increasing his IQ can wait; my desire for my duvet cannot.

'He's just a hungry wee man, a growing lad,' counsels another hopeful helper. 'He'll be fine once he's six months and can go on to solids, you'll see!'

'Hmm,' I agree, dubiously, eyeing the half-empty packet of baby rice hidden behind my dusty breast pump. A full roast might well achieve the desired levels of drowsiness, but a token helping of 'polyfilla' does not appear to be doing the trick.

Oldest Friend – less tact, more truth – is still sympathetic, but entirely unsurprised. 'He doesn't sleep? Well, what do you expect? You're hardly great role models for taking it easy! The FOB sleeps in shifts while he's saving the Western world and you race through life like the Road Runner on Red Bull. What hope has he got of being a great sleeper with parents like *you*?'

I cringe, but reluctantly agree that she probably has a point.

While my son is undoubtedly contented – and who wouldn't be with gold-top on tap? – his mother, on the other hand, is nigh on demented. Rubbing my wrinkles, I finally admit defeat. My malfunctioning manual is passed on to an unsuspecting mum-to-be at the local antenatal sale. And as I hand it over with one hand, and stifle a yawn with the other, I wish her all the luck, and sleep, in the world.

★ ★ ★

Nine months on and the seven-till-seven Holy Grail of slumber continues to swim in front of my now vacuous eyes like an ever-elusive carrot.

A little down, but not out, the FOB and I embark on a last one-boy break in the Scilly Isles, before the imminent arrival of Binary Boy. At eight months pregnant, I am hot, hormonal and frankly huge. I am also absolutely exhausted.

Manual number one has been replaced by manuals two, three and four, each sleep section thumbed and thumbed again in a desperate bid to find the solution to what has become an all-consuming concern. For in defiance of the accepted stats, our cupcake, now turned large muffin, continues to insist that midnight feasts are de rigueur, and that waking later than 5 a.m. means he must surely be missing the best bit of the day.

The going to bed is fine. It's the staying there that's the problem.

And so it is that I find myself, on alternate 'my-turn-to-do-dawn' days, propped awkwardly against an uncomfortable sofa in our St Mary's chalet, squinting into the half-light of the rising summer sun and wondering what to do – quietly – with my good-to-go toddler until such time as is acceptable to wake up his still dead-to-the-world dad.

Always a better eater than sleeper, he finishes breakfast in just five minutes. *Dear Zoo* can occupy another five, ten if I can muster enough enthusiasm and energy for 'And what noise does the lion make?'

Nappy change – good, another ten.

Nearly there.

Nearly . . .

Yes!

Grasping the remote control, I punch in the magic numbers: 71. Ahhh, CBeebies.

To this day, the *Balamory* theme tune can make me feel mildly nauseous, while the appearance of a Teletubby can reduce me to tears. Tears not of despair for their inane elocution, but of joy at the memory of how, for at least the ensuing fifteen minutes or so, I could shut my eyes and drift off to my own lala land while my troublesome toddler sat spellbound, engrossed in the 'uh ohs' of a bunch of coloured blobs.

'Mumma shleepin? Mumma tired?' enquires my son halfway through, thoughtfully prising my eyelids open – just to check.

'No, Mumma's awake,' I mumble, squinting at the clock and despondently noting that only four minutes have elapsed since I last dropped off. 'Oooh, look, where's Tinky Winky gone?' Gratefully, I grab another quick kip while he stares at the screen and endeavours to find out.

Predictably, but unfairly in my opinion, boys numbers two and three follow in their elder brother's nocturnal footsteps, and so the sleep story goes on and on.

Strangers are admiring, but inadvertently exasperating.

'Oooh, what wonderfully energetic boys!' they exclaim at the beach/park/on a ten-mile hike. 'At least after all that fresh air, they'll sleep well tonight!' I turn another yawn into a pained smile. In my unfortunately all-too-extensive experience, the more physically exhausted my boy brood are, the worse they sleep.

Websites provide companionable support, but suggest no solutions.

'Is it just *my* sons who won't sleep through the night?' I tap in one morning, at around twenty to six. The response is immediate, which says something in itself. 'Noooo,' howl a horde of already-up MOBs. The vast majority of the MOGs, presumably, are still tucked up in bed.

So it's back to the drawing board and my army of experts.

I consult manual number five. The ever-practical and refreshingly honest Dr Green confirms what I have, truth be told, begun to fear and suspect. You can bin your blackouts, forget controlled crying, stick to routines as much as you like: for the parents of early birds the prognosis is not good. The cure, it appears, is as elusive as my long-term memory and there is but one way out: accept the inevitable, he suggests sagely, and . . .GO TO BED EARLIER. Ah, the science of rockets. From now on then, we must watch the weather online and not semi-comatose on the sofa, after the news, and after ten.

'Hallelujah!' I cry, suddenly sitting up and thrusting Dr (recently promoted to God) Green under the FOB's drooping eyelids. He struggles from the sheets where he purports to be preparing for another boy-broken night (though quite why he feels the need, I have never understood; it would take a torpedo attack at least to stir him from *his* slumber).

'Look – here, here!' I say, pointing at the liberating lines. 'This manual says there's nothing we can do about the boys not sleeping, if we've tried everything he's suggested . . . that it's just one of those things. Look he says it's OK. He says that we're *normal*!'

My semi-dormant husband raises his eyebrows, struggling to follow my admittedly wayward train of thought. 'Don't you see?' I explain excitedly, 'It's A + B . . . they don't necessarily equal C!'

'Great,' he mutters, plumping up his pillow and turning off his light, 'so we're normal, after all. Now can I please get some kip?'

I am too excited by my new-found freedom to sleep much that night. I suspect that this is not what the God Doctor ordered.

My enthusiastic acceptance of early risers does not last long.

Try as I might, I never quite manage to put myself to bed

before the end of the nightly news. Never quite manage to out the owl and learn, instead, to love the lark.

And so, as first one, then two and, finally, three plaintive cries of 'Mummmmaaaa' join in a distinctly more chirpy dawn chorus, I still struggle to drag my bleary body, brain and at least one baby, out of bed and to the breakfast table on a disappointingly daily basis.

'It's OK though,' I whisper at my reflection, as I pass the mirror on the stairs: porridge-splattered dressing gown, grid-reference wrinkles, defiant pink slippers. 'It's OK because you're *normal.*' My dead-beat mum-mug stares doubtfully back.

A mere three and a half hours, a steaming hot shower and several espressos later, however, and I am ready and respectable enough to face the waiting world.

Or so I believe until I meet 'Bob'. 'Bob' is – to coin the current best-boy phrase, 'Well duh!' – a builder. For while our sizable Renault Scenic can just about accommodate our expanding family, our compact dwelling most definitely cannot.

With hindsight (ahh, there I go again!) and a substantial lottery win, we wouldn't have bought a character-cottage in the first place. Instead, we would have acquired a male-made mansion complete with his and MY bathrooms, sound and bulletproof walls and a garden big enough to wallop a ball in without beheading the buddleia.

However, it's no use crying over misspent mortgages, and thus it is that the FOB and I decide, in our undoubted wisdom, to embark on a fairly substantial extension project. Three boys under four, all insomniac and in tow. Restoration Nightmare?! Beeny, eat your heart out.

Fortunately, we are able to move into a Naval married quarter for what should (in theory) be the majority of the build, while the garden adopts the perilous attributes of the aftermath of a bomb and the house (and its dust-deadened contents) is exposed to the elements of a predictably unpredictable British winter.

One fine day in late August, however, we can put it off no longer. Sensible Son is about to start school. We may have no kitchen, but we also have no choice. We must move back home.

Waving a tearful goodbye to our relatively palatial married quarter we head back: back to our unfortunately *still* scaffolded house, to our unfortunately *still* 'temporary' tip garden, and back, face-to-flippant-face on a daily basis, with 'Bob'.

So. 'Mornin',' I grunt as I bundle my sons out of the back door, after only the aforementioned three and a half hours, steaming hot shower, copious coffees, etc., etc. I tiptoe over the sea of masonry and mud that laps what I'm sure was once (and should *actually* be again by now) our doorstep.

'Just got up, have we?' quips 'Bob', nursing his first (and certainly not last) cup of builder's brew of the day and eyeing my still-sopping hair and just-grabbed clothes.

I force a distinctly cool smile. How can it be that I have been up since first light and, while the boys have faces flannelled, hair flattened and stomachs fed, I still haven't managed to so much as point a hairdryer at my own bedraggled mop?

Just got up, eh? 'That's about as likely as you having finished this project on budget and on *time*,' I quip, under slumber-deprived and building-depraved breath. I force my octopus Feisty Fellow into his buggy and prepare for the almost inevitable school *run*. Unperturbed, 'Bob' slurps on.

I am halfway down the lane before 'Bob' shouts. 'Stop . . . hey, stop!'

'What is it now?' I retort, mid-flight, eyeing him with over-inflated infuriation as he automatically replaces his first tea with first tab.

Grinning, he points helpfully at my feet. I look down.

'What?' I shoot back at him, daring him to comment on my inadvertently unusual choice of footwear.

'Nothing . . .' he backs down, suddenly unwilling to push this mad mother any further than he already has. 'Nothing.' Instead, he takes a loooong drag on his fag.

Interestingly, no one else remarks on my pink slippers at school, and indeed I notice that many other mothers are wearing equally fashionable fur-lined boots. And only the word 'UGG' is missing from mine. I rub the sleep from my eyes and smile. It feels good to be somehow part of a trend.

'Bob' eventually leaves the building some three months later than scheduled. The duvet deprivation takes substantially longer to fix.

A mere *eight* years – yes, take heart, fellow MOBs, there *is* an end to your tunnel of tiredness – down the sleep-slashed line, a minor miracle has finally come to pass. Because Feisty Fellow has learned his 'numbas' and is now able to abide by the previously entirely unattainable 'silence till seven' subsection C.

And Binary Boy has learned how to operate the remote control, has discovered that there is more to Freeview than Josie Jump and has even been known to quietly negotiate (rather than loudly dictate) the appropriate choice of early-morning entertainment.

Meanwhile, Sensible Son has become amazingly adept at the removal of the plastic protector from a carton of full-fat, thereby mastering the thus-far elusive art of the self-service Shreddie.

And so our long-running nocturnal nightmare seems to have come to an end.

I donate God Green and the remaining band of merry manuals to the 'bring-and-buy' book stall at the local school fete. I substitute my espressos with one long, languid latte, downed indulgently in bed, and with only the *Today* team to keep me company. And I finally replace the rusting batteries in my till-now redundant alarm clock with some brand spanking new Duracell bunnies.

Because the other day I found myself asleep – yes, actually ASLEEP – at the ungodly and potentially fatal hour of *8 a.m.*

'Why didn't you wake me?' I scream at my no-longer nocturnal sons, as I frantically butter bread for their schoolboy sarnies. Three faces stare at me bewildered, as if I'm talking in tongues, before returning their gazes to the serenity of the screen.

Needless to say, the too-short morning is carnage and we only just make it to school on time . . . but who cares?

'Sorry we're a bit late,' I prattle excessively to the teacher on the gate. 'It's just that we, well . . . I' – I pause dramatically here, committing the moment to memory – '*overslept!*'

'Oh, don't worry!' she replies cheerily. 'It happens to us all once in a while, doesn't it? It's perfectly normal!'

I stare at her, ridiculously, deliriously delighted. 'Normal?! Yes . . . isn't it just? Wonderfully, perfectly normal.'

The top ten reads by every MOB's bed

- *Cool Camping* (Punk Publishing) – well read
- *Cool Camping Kids* (Punk Publishing) – extremely well read
- Luxury spa holiday brochure – unopened
- *Mountainous Meals in Minutes for No Money*
- Countless MOB manuals – well thumbed, but dusty
- *Five Minutes' Peace* (Jill Murphy)
- An atlas
- Top Trumps
- Confessions of a Yummy/Slummy/Scummy Mummy (hormone dependent)
- Absolutely nothing – too tired to read

The top ten reads by every FOB's bed

- *Build It!*
- *The Dangerous Book for Boys* (Conn & Hal Iggulden)
- *Mr Large In Charge* (again the insightful and amusing Jill Murphy)
- ScrewFix catalogue
- Complete DIY manual
- *Football / Rugby / Golf* (insert any sport here) *for Absolute Experts*
- *Massage for Beginners* – strategically placed by the MOB, completely ignored by the FOB
- The unabridged collection of *Thomas the Tank Engine* (The Rev. W. Awdry)
- Operating instructions for a Dyson
- No books – just a mobile phone with a flatulent App

The top ten reads by a little boy's bed

- *Monkey Puzzle* (Julia Donaldson & Axel Scheffler)
- *How to Avoid a Wombat's Bum* (Mitchell Symons)
- *The Best of Jennings* (Anthony Buckeridge)
- *The Circus / Island* (/ anything) *of Adventure* (Enid Blyton)
- Anything and everything by Dick King-Smith
- *You Choose* (Nick Sharratt & Pippa Goodhart)
- *National Geographic Kids*
- *Badness for Beginners* (Ian Whybrow & Tony Ross)
- *Where's Wally?* (Martin Handford)
- *Charlie and* (of course) *the Chocolate Factory* (Roald Dahl)

The Demented Little Lady Routine (for three boys under four)

18:30   Bath (warm water mixed with several glugs of lavender oil; it says 'sleep inducing' on the bottle – worth a try).

18:45   Take baby out of bath. Lay on towel for some nappy-free time. Persuade toddler out of bath and dress. Soak up pee from beneath nappy-free infant. Dress baby and lay in cot for a kick.

18:50   Read to toddler. Interrupt to pick up now crying baby. Read to toddler with baby in arms. Kiss toddler goodnight: 'See you in the morning!' As if.

18:55   Dry, dress and read to eldest son. Baby now starving – eldest son can't hear his book. Bring forward baby's (in theory) last feed of the day; baby under one arm, book in the other. Baby falls asleep almost immediately. Finish reading. Kiss eldest son goodnight: 'See you in the morning!' Well, you never know.

19:00   Place comatose baby in cot and rapidly retreat. Whisper: 'See you later.' (You may be optimistic, but you're not totally deranged.)

21:30   Fall asleep in front of TV with now back-from-work FOB. Wake up for the weather and then stagger to bed.

22:30–

01:00   Silence.

01:01   Baby whimpers. Hear, but ignore.

01:04   Baby cries. Hear, but hope he'll settle himself.

01:06   Leap out of bed as baby goes for it full throttle. Grab him before he wakes his siblings and dad. Sink into chair, plug him in, nod off.

01:08	Eldest son pulls sleeve of pyjamas. '*He* woke me up!' 'Never mind, go back to bed.' 'Can't!' 'Why?' 'Can't find Teddy!' Return once-again-out-for-the-count baby to cot. Find Teddy down side of eldest son's bed. 'See you in the morning!' Zombie back to bed.
01:15	Someone's screaming. Leap out of bed. It's middle son: a nightmare. Soothe back to sleep and tiptoe away. 'See you in the morning!' Trudge back to bed. The FOB is snoring, not loudly, but just enough to irritate. Kick FOB.
01:25 –	
04:45	Silence.
04:46	Baby crying. Squint at clock, switch off baby monitor (why *do* we still have one when you can hear him through the wall?) and leap out of bed. (If you don't get to him within seconds, he'll wake the whole house. And that will be the end of the night as you know it.)
04:47 –	
05:20	Silence.
05:21	Wake, cold, to find self sitting in chair with boob hanging out. Baby fast asleep on lap. Put baby in cot. Surrender. Slop downstairs to make first cup of tea.
07:00	The FOB bounds into kitchen. His sons are sitting at the table demolishing porridge. You are sitting next to them, staring into space. The FOB: 'Just what I needed . . . a good night's kip . . . I don't know about you, but I slept like a log!' Hand the FOB a mug of tepid tea, and head back to bed.

LESSON 3:

More balls than most

I discovered only the other day that the potty comes in both boy and girl versions.

I am flabbergasted.

Not so much by the need for it – fairly sensible really, when you think about it, a receptacle with differing depths of 'lip' – as by the fact that the existence of gender-specific potties had thus far escaped my attention. Because I was (so *I* thought) reasonably expert in all matters bottom, and those in any way pertaining to pee.

But it's been twelve days now. Two hundred and eighty-eight hours. Or 17,280 son-speak minutes. (Unlike the male members of my family, I am of the female variety and thus have approximately zero interest in working out exactly how long that equates to in seconds.) And I have to admit that I am almost starting to get withdrawal symptoms – that I'm even, *almost,* beginning to miss them. After all, it has been very nearly *nine* years since I started my long, deep, if not always entirely mean-ingful, relationship with my male offspring and, by definition, their boy 'bits'.

In the beginning, the relationship was of a fairly predictable and practical nature. What goes in, of course, has to come out and when it does, it needs attending to. Swiftly *and* skilfully, immediately . . . or else. Or it'll be you, not just him, who is in the proverbial.

We learned the hard way.

When the nurses showed me how in hospital it seemed pretty straightforward. Flat on his back and newborn docile, my first-born son had been completely compliant. I lifted his legs, cleaned his crevices and cracks, and swaddled him quickly in a doll-sized diaper. No fuss, no mess, as easy as pie. Unfortunately pie comes before a fall.

At two days old, the FOB and I take our brand-new baby home. We deposit him in his car seat on our bedroom floor.

'What do we do now?' asks the FOB.

I stare at our sleeping son. Shrug. 'Not sure.'

'Surely we must have to do *something*?' he says.

'Like what?'

He shrugs. 'Not sure.'

In the end we lie down on the bed – just for a second – to decide what to do.

We are awoken ten minutes later as he starts to cry. We jump up and look down at our now bawling baby.

'What does he want?' asks the FOB.

I stare at our infant. Shrug. 'Not sure.'

'Is he hungry?' asks my husband again, for whom food is the answer to most of life's problems.

'Don't think so. I only fed him half an hour ago.'

'Is he cold?'

I gesture towards the mountains of blankets in which we have cocooned our child.

'Hot, then?'

I look at our son's disgruntled face; at the bulge between his legs. 'Nooo . . . I think he needs changing.'

Operation 'nappy change' swings into action. The FOB de-Babygros the baby while I fetch the equipment: changing mat, wipes and a freshly folded nappy. We kneel down beside our son and prepare for the 'off'.

This is his – and our – first poo.

It is black, it is sticky and there is rather a lot of it.

'Is that normal?' grimaces the FOB, wrinkling his nose.

'Not sure,' I answer. I can't recall my manuals having pictures of *this*.

'How can so much be done so swiftly by one so small?' misquotes the FOB, eyeing the meconium snake, apparently without end. I deploy yet another wodge of wipes in an ineffectual attempt to stem the flow.

After what seems like for ever, the serpent stops.

'You need to make sure he's really clean,' I instruct my never-changed-a-nappy-before husband. 'That's right . . . get it all off . . . and under there.' Gingerly, he lifts his son's still overblown appendages and peers closely to check for lingering bits.

At this precise moment, our infant chooses to remind us that he was born BOY.

His willy – previously passive – leaps into action and a geyser of pee shoots into the air. Missing the changing mat entirely, it soaks everything and everyone within a five-foot radius.

I dive for safety behind the bed, but the FOB, unfortunately, is not fast enough on his feet.

This is *one* mistake he won't be making again.

Some nine weeks later, the FOB is just about over the 'willy wash' incident. A pile of cut-up old sheets is on constant standby by the side of the mat, and we are sufficiently confident of our parental prowess to take our firstborn out in public. We have been invited to attend a family wedding.

Picture the scene: bride resplendent, groom gleaming, guests elegant, sun shining.

And then there's me: a battered, shattered, somewhat shell-shocked MOB.

Thus far, my daily wardrobe switches between stretchy pyjamas and panelled trousers. Some days it doesn't even switch at all. But, as befits this auspicious occasion, I have invested in an expensive off-white tent, which I trust will conceal my still sag-bag stomach, but which is, it seems, merely leaving bemused (and it has to be said, mostly male) members of the marital party wondering whether I've already given birth or am still in a state of antenatal suspense.

'Well . . . congratulations. I didn't know you were expecting!' cries one – I like to think short-sighted – guest, eyeing my belly with the polite interest of one who has been told by his wife he should comment on such things. I cough and redden, unsure of quite how to respond without either a) bursting into tears or b) causing him untold embarrassment. 'When's it due?' he continues, plonking his well-buffed foot even more firmly in it.

'I . . . I . . .' I falter, instinctively trying – and failing miserably – to suck my tell-tale tummy back to anything veering towards the vertical. We face each other in an uncomfortable impasse.

'Darling, ah, here you are. Sorry to interrupt,' the dapper FOB bursts on to the scene, 'but I think he's hungry!' He thrusts our baby into my waiting arms. Sensible Son snuffles frantically for sustenance like a calf on a cow.

I smile, part sympathetic, part victorious at my now mortified friend.

'I . . . well . . . well, well done you! A baby boy . . . how wonderful. Wonderful!' he splutters, before hotfooting it to the pub for a pre-service swift one. 'And you don't even look like you've just had a baby,' he throws over his shoulder, trying, I presume, to dig himself out of his increasingly insulting hole.

Clutching my baby to my over-inflated bosom, I set off in search of a shady spot where I can feed my son, and lick my womanly wounds, in peace.

The subsequent timing of my infant-accessory is impeccable.

We are making our way over the cobbles towards the church door, where we will take our places in the pew and await the arrival of the bride, when IT happens.

To the untrained ear, it starts out sounding like a steam train, rumbling away innocently enough in the distance. Mere moments later, however, the train transmogrifies into a moisture-ridden firework which fails to entirely explode: a promising whoosh followed swiftly by a squidgy-sounding 'phwart'.

To my marginally more attuned – but blatantly not *pre*-attuned enough – oracle, and when combined with the damp sensation spreading in a southerly direction down the front of my dress, this Thomas Tank turned roving rocket spells trouble. With an upper-case T.

Too late, I hold my son away from my body, and check the damage. The undulating folds of cream fabric have been replaced by a son-slick of disastrous proportions.

'Whoops,' understates the FOB, gingerly taking the proffered baby, and holding him, and his enthusiastically acquired environmentally friendly (but apparently not poo-proof) 'natural nappy', at a safe extra-long arm's length.

'Indeed,' I say through teeth more gritted than a country lane on a winter's morn. I lay the baby bag on top of a convenient headstone and delve inside for emergency equipment. Thrusting a disposable nappy, a handful of wipes and the 'we've-learned-from-experience anti-willy wash cloths' at my husband, I direct father and son to the nearest sanitising spot. Pulling out the rest of the Johnsons (fragrance-free), I embark on my own clean-up campaign.

But this slick is, now obviously, *not* for the stopping.

Ten minutes later, my now be'Pampered son reappears, immaculate in another outfit from his extensive wedding wardrobe. I, on the other hand, have a tent, one tent and nothing but. So help me, FOB.

Close to tears, I eye my midriff with dismay; a dull ochre blob bleeds like ink on blotting paper, and the deployment of wipes has merely made matters worse. I look up in despair at my statuesque spouse.

'I'm going to have to wear your jacket over the top!'

He shivers, but nods chivalrously.

'Here you go,' says my towering husband, hanging his jacket on to my substantially slighter shoulders. 'Perfect!'

'Harrumph!' I sulk, pulling ineffectually at the outsized garment. 'Harrumph!'

But it appears that every cloud – even a malodorous one – has its own silver lining. For the jacket, it turns out, leaves me blessed in disguise.

'Oooh, look at your wee one . . . he's so sweet, so adorable!' coo an appreciative army of ageing aunts. 'And look at you: so slim already. Why, your clothes are positively hanging off you!'

I bask happily in their compliments. 'No more expensive investments in supposedly attractive attire,' I whisper in the ear of the now frozen FOB. 'I'll be raiding *your* wardrobe from now on.' An uncertain smile hovers round his ever-so-slightly blue lips.

And so the years pass quickly, and as first one and then two more bouncing boy bums join our merry throng, my intimate understanding of boys' bodies, and how to deal with them, increases accordingly.

Three boys, three sets of bits.

Like painting the Firth of Forth Bridge, nappy-changing sessions take on the nightmarish feel of a rollercoaster ride which, fight as you might, you just can't seem to get off.

Half-caught conversations are indefinitely interrupted as the whiff of yet another son's status reaches my over-sensitive nose. The window ledge in the kitchen is hidden under a hopeful array of moisturising miracle creams, none of which can save my wash-wizened hands. And as the sitting room simmers with eau de 'Sustainably Drying Nappy', I begin to appreciate the appeal of the disposable diaper.

Heavy of heart, soiled of hand and with the tumble dryer down the garden in the pre-extension shed – by bum number three, I finally give in. My beloved natural nappies go the way of my less appreciated mothering manuals. I hand them over sadly to one more able and willing to wash, and I return, once again, to the supermarket shelves.

But nappies (and even willy wash – although I suspect here the FOB might well beg to differ) are – I realise belatedly – at the easier end of the dealing-with-boy-bits spectrum. Getting boys out of them, on to and – dare I dream it? – weeing *into* the loo, involves whole new echelons of anatomical expertise.

It's summertime.

No need for poppers, pants or even, at a push, clothes. The ideal time, therefore, to embark on potty training. Or so I, MOB-mistakenly, thought.

We spend most of our days outside in the garden. An older family friend comes round for tea and I greet her by her car.

'You'll have to excuse Sensible Son,' I say, nodding towards my starkers child as he zooms down the slide. 'We're potty training!'

She watches, and winces. 'Oh . . . um . . . right,' she says. 'And, er, how is it going?'

'Well,' I say, '*really* well. We haven't done a wee in our pants since Tuesday, and we've only had one accident at night.' I fail to notice her 'enough-information' look and continue, 'Though he still prefers peeing against trees to using the potty.' (Aha – so *that*, I realise suddenly, is why gender-specific potties slipped under my radar!) 'Oh, and we're struggling a *little* with number twos on the loo.'

I've blatantly gone beyond her decency bounds.

She coughs. 'Aren't your flowers looking lovely?'

I refuse to be derailed from my current potty-training preoccupation. 'It must be all the extra ammonia they're getting at the moment!' I reply, laughing.

We head to the table for coffee and cake.

Later that afternoon, we are still sitting in the sunshine catching up on news. Binary Boy trundles round the garden pushing a trolley of bricks and Sensible Son . . . Actually, where is he? I realise I haven't seen him for some time, and while the gate is shut so he can't have escaped, any kind of silence does not usually bode well. Family Friend and I leave our cake crumbs and embark on a search.

It doesn't take long.

'He's over here,' calls out Family Friend. 'I can see his feet behind that bush!' I hurry over to where she is pointing.

'There you are,' I say mildly relieved. 'What *are* you doing behind there . . . urgh . . . oh.'

Sensible Son is squatting, wide of eye and bushy of tail, beside a rose bush. He's mid-manure.

'Is he all right?' asks Family Friend, mercifully far from the scene of the crime.

'He's fine, fine . . . um, we're just popping into the house for a moment or two.'

I clean up my boy and put him back in a pull-up.

Two weeks later I've got it sussed. Well, sort of.

Sensible Son is now enthusiastically adept at using the loo for a poo, and can see the attractions of a toilet – not a tree – for a wee. But while the *will* is there, the *willy* – and the mind that is its own – is too. Ergo, while my son may be teetering on 'dry', the carpets which surround the toilets are not.

Fellow MOBs advise ping-pong ball 'target training'. We try it – once.

'See if you can sink it!' I encourage, as he stands by the pan and carefully takes aim. 'That's it!' I cry as he bombards the ball. Could it be that this – frankly odd – approach to precision peeing might actually *work*?

Binary Boy totters into the bathroom to see what all the fuss is about. Spying the target, and before I can stop him, he reaches into the toilet bowl and fishes it out.

'*Ball*,' he states proudly, dripping it dry.

So instead, the house continues to ring to my none-too-dulcet tones:

'I know it points up, but can't you just push it *down*?'

'How on earth did you manage to get *that* up *there*?'

'Will you watch what you're doing, and wee *in* the loo!'

And the carpets continue to ever so slightly hum.

Thus far, I have perhaps given the impression that my relationship with my boys' bits is based almost exclusively upon trial and trauma. To leave it at that, however, would be to paint only part of the picture.

Because actually, I love them. Particularly their bottoms: peachy, bare and preferably on the beach. I adore the way they dimple when they sit on the sand. How they wobble when they toddle and tumble in the waves. The way they squidge and squirm when you rub-a-dub-dub them free of salty water, before plonking themselves happily on to your waiting (now wet) knee.

In the right place, at the right time, you'd struggle to beat a good boy bum.

Unfortunately for my lads and their backsides – and may I be so bold as to suggest, for the majority of males – they fail to understand that even their mostly bottom-besotted mother can have too much of a good thing. My (over)extensive exposure to flatulence merely goes to prove my point.

It had gone unnoticed in Sensible Son and Binary Boy, and indeed at first, with Feisty Fellow, we put it down to wind. The oh-so-polite 'poop!' followed by an almost imperceptible smile: at just two months old, the baby's occasional love puffs and subsequent gummy grin caused little excitement in our fart-familiar house.

As time passed, however, it became obvious that the giggles which accompanied each tiny trumpet were more than an involuntary reaction to a natural bodily function.

At five months old, and propped up against the sofa, our cherub rapidly became an expert at entertaining an audience. Cooing loudly to ensure our undivided attention, our ne'er-so-innocent infant would stare into the middle distance, casually raise one buttock . . . and let out an extra-loud rip-roaring fart. 'Wind' played no part in these perfect performances.

At twelve months, he continued to perfect his technique.

With every instance of flatulence, his jelly belly would wobble delightedly at both the sounds, and now the smells, he was able to achieve. Chortling like Churchill, he'd watch as his elder brothers would collapse in heaps of hyena hysteria, rendered virtually speechless – and breathless – by his fragrant foibles.

'He parted! He parted!' Sensible Son would chant delightedly, while Binary Boy raced round the room like a demented dog.

The FOB and I would stare at each other, wondering what tack – if any – to take.

In the interests of decency (and for the benefit of our neighbours) I'd try to intervene.

'Will you calm down please, boys,' I'd bewail. 'It's only natural. Everyone does it – it's not *that* funny!'

But my MOB protestations fell on deaf ears. And so the fart-fuelled fun went onwards . . . and up?

The government's (and my own) five-a-day fixation ensured that we had an almost constant supply of poop-induced mirth. On the beach, parping 'nudey' was particularly popular and astonishingly loud. Squished in the car, letting rip provided sometimes almost welcome relief from I spy and . . . I spy. Pristine, pyjama-clad and ready for sleep, trumping prolonged the bed-going process by half an hour or more, as I wrestled to re-impose a guff-free zone.

Farts, to this melee of men, and despite my claims to the contrary, were funny.

It is at the dinner table that whatever even faintly amusing aspects there might conceivably be to flatulence finally fall, well . . . flat.

With just four activity-infested weeks to go before the Christmas holidays, the boys sit down at the table for supper, while I frantically mix yet another bleedin' 'bake a cake for class'.

I try to blank out their competing catcalls while they practise – ever louder – for their nativity roles.

'I was singing first!' shrieks Binary Boy.

'But I'm Joseph. I'm more important than you,' sneers Sensible Son. 'You're just a *shepherd*!'

'I'm best of all, isn't I, Mummy?' squeals their youngest brother. 'Cos I'm a pig!'

I sigh, beat even harder and reflect on the inadvertent injustices of life. *My* life where, as a multiple MOB, I must procure pink tights, a pink top and a curly pink tail. Why couldn't he be a cow, I grumble unreasonably into my mixture. Or a shepherd, like his brother? Brown I could do and we've tea towels aplenty . . . but *pink*?

Anyway.

'That's enough singing for the moment, thank you, boys,' I say, slopping cake mixture into cases, 'just get on and eat – please!'

A (temporary) silence reigns.

The silence is broken as I turn my back – for a split second – to put my educational offerings into the oven.

'What's that smell?' moans one unidentifiable son.

'Pooooeyy . . . who was *that*?' groans another.

'I did it, I did it. It was me, was *my* part!' chants what turns out to be my youngest perpetrator proudly.

'You stinker! You skunk!' rejoice his too-impressed siblings, egging him unnecessarily and mercilessly on.

Rising to the occasion, Feisty Fellow jumps to his feet. Wobbling precariously on the edge of his chair, he wiggles his bottom in his siblings' fascinated faces. Silently praying that this finale may indeed constitute the end of the event, I hold my tongue. But there's more. Excited by his brothers' now tear-inducing enthusiasm, Feisty Fellow grapples with his (unfortunately elasticated) trousers, before going through the motions of the fullest of Montys.

His bare bottom hangs over the tea table like a very full moon.

'That's enough!' I yell, breaking that day's latest MOB resolution to talk calmly, *not* shout.

The defiant derrière wiggles even more wildly than before.

'I said: that's enough!' I admonish again, trying desperately to keep my cool and not let the boys sense, or worse, see, the smile which hovers unbidden and unhelpfully at the corners of my mouth.

My boys, unfortunately, are obviously more empathetic than I have previously surmised. Sensing a chink in their mother's disciplinary armour, the older two now take to their feet too. In an unwitting tribute to The Tweets, they perform their very own Birdie Song, flashing their flesh to an imaginary beat. Completely out of control now and deaf to my half-hearted protests, they party on.

'What on *earth* is going on in here?'

As one, the twits stop twirling, mid-tweet. The return of the FOB.

'Thank goodness you're home early for once!' I say, throwing my arms around him. He raises one eyebrow towards his semi-naked sons, eyeing the unexplained dining-room devastation.

'Don't ask!' I say. 'Could you just take them upstairs for a bath please? I'm not sure I can face any more exposure to flesh – or feathers – tonight!'

He eyes me oddly. 'Sure. Come on boys, time for a bath . . . and can you put your pants on before we all go up? You're at the tea table now you know, not the beach!'

Grinning, the boys obediently re-robe and follow their father.

'So what did you do at nursery today?' I hear my husband ask Feisty Fellow, halfway up the stairs.

'He's been doing rhyming words, haven't you?' interjects Binary Boy.

'Have you really? Rhyming – brilliant. So, young man,' chuckles my in-theory adult other half, as I – suddenly fearful – listen in, 'what rhymes with "cart"?'

Overhead, three small boys and one substantially larger one morph into elephants of chaos.

Gently but firmly, I pull the sitting-room door to, before pouring myself an extra-large bucket of calming Chianti.

But it's been twelve days now. Twelve days since I've been up close and personal with my growing-up boys' bits.

Because eventually, of course, and after much pooing and froing, all three boys are dry. Eventually, of course, the boys improve (if not perfect) the precision pee. And eventually, of course – although this takes ludicrously longer than it realistically should – cries of 'I've finnnnnnnisssssssshed' are finally replaced by a self-sufficient wipe.

OK, so a fart is still the funniest thing since Perfect Peter. Oh, and the seat's always up. And they never, EVER flush the loo. But even *I* know when I'd be asking too much of my mini-men.

The house smells surprisingly fresh and is, at times, almost eerily quiet. My hands, of course, will never recover, but I wear my motherly wash-wrinkles with pride. For this MOB has faced her fears, their farts and a plethora of posteriors . . . and she has survived.

Post-'Bob' and his extended extension, we get an estate agent round to value the house. Just in case we can ever afford *that* mansion with the sound- and bullet-proofed walls. We arrive at what is now the dedicated kids' bathroom.

'Nice fittings,' he says, admiring the chrome. His eyes skim the rest of the room. He stops at the loo.

'Oh, yeah . . . sorry. Boys, hey? They appear to be *incapable* of putting the toilet seat down.'

'Err, no, it's not so much that, Mrs Evans, but . . . ahem . . . do you have any problems with your plumbing?'

I look horrified into the toilet bowl . . . and blush as *I* flush.

Essential strategies for living with boys' bits

- Install industrial drains with minimal U-bends.
- Ration toilet paper.
- Indoctrinate boys early on that the loo seat stays down.
- Put laminate down in the bathroom. Actually, throughout the house.
- Ensure that your boys have both hands on *top* of the duvet *before* you embark on a bedtime story.
- Buy one of those weird-looking ping-pong balls with a funny face on it and pop it in the loo. It will confuse the hell out of the MOGs, but your lads will love it!
- If at all possible, invest in an en suite.
- Accept that pulling down your pants means the same to a male as a 'high five' does to his female friends.
- Willies are wonderful and farting is funny. No, really. They are.

While farting is fascinating, boys go wild for their willies. But even this male obsession can be put to good use by a manipulative MOB.

The Beetroot and Chocolatey Bribery Cake

Step 1: Take one boy.
Step 2: Take one beetroot and suggest that eating beetroot is good for boy.
Step 3: Ignore Charlie-and-Lola look of horror and disgust. He will never ever eat a beetroot.
Step 4: Get him to bet you 10p that if he eats the beetroot, his pee will turn pink. Shake on it.
Step 5: Get out your mixer and start on this cake.

Preparation time: 20 minutes (assuming you're alone, without your jumble of Jamies)
Cooking time: 1–1¼ hours (assuming the oven's left shut and the cake's not continually checked)
Serves: 8 (assuming no one has been putting his fingers in your bowl); more realistically then, 6

Ingredients
250g self-raising flour	200g beetroot, grated
50g cocoa	100g sultanas
2 tsp baking powder	150ml vegetable oil
150g soft brown sugar	2 medium eggs, beaten

The MOB method
1. Preheat the oven to 160° C/gas 3/fan oven 140° C. Butter and line the base of a 20cm round cake tin.
2. Sift flour, cocoa and baking powder into a large bowl and stir in soft brown sugar. Add the grated beetroot and sultanas.
3. In a separate bowl, beat together the oil and eggs. Add to the dry ingredients. Mix well.
4. Spoon mixture into prepared tin. Bake in preheated oven for 1–1¼ hours, until a skewer inserted into the middle of the cake comes out clean.
5. Cool in the tin for 10 minutes, then turn out on to a wire rack and leave to cool completely.
6. Wait for beetroot and appropriate accompanying drink to take effect. Assess the evidence, hand over 10p, but then sit back, smug. 'Oh yes, *my* boy will willingly eat all his fruit *and* his veg!'

Treat your male like a mastiff and you won't go far wrong

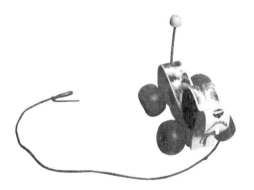

In the time since I first set eyes on Sensible Son, I have come to the conclusion that bringing up boys is like dealing with dogs.

And whether your male is the cutest chihuahua, the gangliest Great Dane or even, gawd help you, a bare-bottomed boxer, his needs – and that of his canine equivalent – are, fundamentally speaking, exactly the same.

Your boy pup needs feeding: hearty helpings of tender tucker, at least (if not more than) three times a day.

He needs a tree, a fence or frankly anything vertical, on which to 'mark his territory' (although in the absence of the above, a toilet *may* suffice).

He needs authority: clear commands of no more than one syllable: 'Stop!' 'No!' 'Now!'

And he needs love: sporadic, manic displays of tummy-tickling torture. (This will, naturally, lead to a riot which will, in all probability, end in tears. But sometimes, fellow females, it's just got to be done.)

However, most, *most* importantly, your furry friend needs walkies. To go out. To let off steam and, perchance, cause a stink. Twice a day, every day, come rain or shine. Or – be warned – it will be you, not just him, who is climbing the walls.

I could chart my progress from one-pup mum to Barbara Woodhouse in many weird and wonderful ways.

I could count the number of minutes I'm permitted to stand in that steaming hot shower before one of my litter bursts through the door with tales of woe, deep injustice and, occasionally, pain.

I could work out how many times I've barked 'Be careful!' at my boys, only to belatedly realise that there's actually no point. 'Careful!' has two syllables, so 'Down!' must do.

Alternatively, and less productively, I could try to add up the occasions on which well-meaning passers-by have eyed me and my pack with an expression I can't always read, before gushing (most often admiringly, occasionally offensively): 'Three boys . . . oh my . . . I just don't know how you do it!'

On a good day, I flash them my well-practised non-committal Mona Lisa smile, which I hope translates as, 'Oh, it's not so bad really!' or, 'At least I don't need to diet!' Or even – on a *very* good day – 'I wouldn't have it any other way!'

On a bad day, typically Monday–Friday, around 8.35 a.m., when I am packing lunches, school bags and mental punches, and my trio are scrabbling at the door like dogs desperate to get out for their morning pee, any attempts at translation are quite frankly, superfluous. 'What else can I do?' I say through barely brushed teeth. 'We made our bed of boys and now we must lie in it . . . for some of the night, at any rate. And anyway,' I shout over my shoulder as we fly down the road to school, 'if you think *these* times are tough, you should've seen me in the olden days!'

The now worried well-wishers begin to regret their off-the-cuff interest, turn on their heels and wend their way.

Ahhh, the 'olden days'. A time when, in the absence of pre-school, big school or any other sanity-saving educational establishment, I had my three barely-more-than-baby boys by my side all day, every day and much of the night. With the FOB at best, at work, and at worst, away on deployment, I had my offspring all to my sleep-deprived and scary self.

In those days, McDonald's wasn't the only establishment open 24/7.

Normal folk, I have since been informed by (it has to be said) mainly MOGs, would have gone to ground. Battened down the hatches. Built themselves a sanctuary and remained well and truly within the confines of its reassuring ramparts. Stayed inside, played inside, shopped online.

But, as this trainee Woodhouse was even then aware, my lad litter didn't overly much appreciate 'inside'. Sure, they'd paint paper for a while before painting each other, watch TV for a bit till they'd all switch off. Occasionally, I'd get out a game and give it a go; we'd throw a couple of sixes, before someone sat on the board. Somehow I couldn't see *us* staying home playing hairdressers and so, for me and my boys, 'out' way back when was absolutely the new 'in'.

We set off in search of out-of-house adventure.

First stop, the supermarket.

Supermarket trolleys – never particularly compliant at the best of times – are, I quickly discover, not designed with me in mind. Tackling the various options and their permutations is a bit like drawing an extremely complicated Venn diagram. And maths (added to science) is not my strongest subject.

'If I put the baby in the car-seat section, and the toddler in the chair . . . hang on, there is no chair-and-car-seat version. Hmmm . . . If I put the baby and toddler in the dual-chair version, then Sensible Son can go . . . Oh, blast – the toddler will never fit in that bucket seat, and even if he did, he'd poke the baby's eyes out. Right, if I put the baby on my back, the toddler in the chair and Sensible Son in the trolley, that could *just* work. OK, off we go!'

I'm halfway down the fruit and veg aisle, buying yet another week's supply of cucumber and carrots and silently praying that the babe on my back will continue to sleep long enough for me to nip to the nappies, that Binary Boy won't get sick from using the undoubtedly germ-ridden trolley bar as a teether and that Sensible Son will complete this supermarket sweep without having to drop his supposedly potty-trained pants, when a lady belonging to the supermarket taps me firmly on the shoulder.

'Excuse me, madam,' she says politely but severely. 'I'm afraid *he*' – looking pointedly at my oldest son who is standing in the trolley downing handfuls of grapes – 'shouldn't be in *there*. It's health and safety,' she adds helpfully. 'He could hurt himself if he fell out.'

I look at her concerned but entirely unempathetic face, imagining for a moment what she would think of his fondness for using our wooden banisters as an impromptu helter-skelter. I'm not at all sure she'd agree with my experiential learning approach.

'Thank you for letting me know,' I say in what I hope is a suitably contrite, yet responsible-mother manner, before gripping the trolley and racing for the raspberries.

Flung forward by my unexpected eagerness, Binary Boy bangs his teeth on the bar and begins to howl. Feisty Fellow raises his formerly floppy head and starts to grumble.

Sensible Son jigs up and down.

'Mummmmy, I need a wee,' he informs me superfluously.

Oh God.

'Right. Sit down quick and we'll find you a loo!' I instruct my eldest, deciding that health and safety can – unlike my children – wait, and that sitting down is *almost* as good as getting out. He plonks himself into the trolley crushing bananas and breadsticks. I look down at the defunct produce in mute despair and notice a spider's-web stain weaving its wicked way across the front of his trousers.

I stifle the urge to remonstrate with my now distraught son –
'My trousers is wet!' – remembering instead, the ambitious
advice on pages 14–15 of manual three: 'Potty Training for
Perfect Parents'.

'Don't worry, it's not the end of the world. It was just an
accident!' I mutter, as much in an attempt to convince myself as
my eldest that this is, indeed, the case.

Leaving the supermarket lady in my frantic wake and ignoring
the Paddington Bear stares of fellow – less encumbered – shop-
pers, we hotfoot it to the checkout. I skid to a stop in front of
the till.

'Do you need any help packing?' asks the cashier. I suspect
that he's as anxious to see the back of me and my bawling brood
as I am of him and his supermarket's obsession with health and
safety. Sensible Son disappears from sight under a sea of bags and
I screwball my way towards the door.

I call in to the local garage for nappies on the way home. For
reasons of health and sanity, I leave my sons locked – safely – in
the car.

One week later and my befuddled brain is ready to try again.

Hurrying past the sweat-inducing supermarket, double buggy
in front and baby on the back, I set off this time for my inaugural
experience of 'Mother Body Beautiful: kids play, while you
puff!'

Perfect, I think to myself, wondering vaguely whether I am
more attracted by the idea of toning up my resolutely beanbag
belly or by having an hour away from my kids.

No matter; Body Beautiful, here we come!

Panting already with the exertion of our arrival, I heave open
the glass door, letting a burst of frozen air into the overheated
porch of the church hall. Inside, I am met by what looks and

sounds like a sea of grannies. And not just any old grannies. No, these are (like Dr Green before) God-sent. God-sent grannies who are, it would appear, prepared – nay, desperate – to relieve me of my burden of boys. All of them.

'You run along next door,' they say cheerfully, 'we'll look after the boys for you. Put the little one over there in the rocker . . . that's right. We'll be fine won't we, chaps, while Mummy goes and does some keep fit? Off you go dear, enjoy yourself!'

This grateful MOB doesn't need to be told twice. Relishing my new-found freedom, I plant a kiss on the heads of my sons and sprint – positively sprint – into the hall. Breathing heavily, I take my place at the back.

Five minutes later, I'm in the middle of painfully stretching my hamstrings and pre-pregnancy Lycra, when a face appears at the window. A familiar face. And it's not happy.

I trot apologetically out of the class towards Sensible Son.

'What's up?' I puff.

'I want to go on the blue bike!' he says.

I look at the room, filled with empty bikes – red – and only one blue. And the blue one is currently occupied by his younger brother.

'Well, why don't you go on a red bike? Red is your favourite colour, isn't it?'

'No,' he says, 'blue's my favourite colour. I want the blue bike.'

Of course you do.

'I tell you what, I'll time how long it takes you to go round the room on a red bike, OK? I bet it's faster than the blue one.'

I fear that this competitive tactic may well come back and bite me on the bottom, but right now it's getting rid of my gluteus maximus I'm worried about, rather than protecting it, so I plump for the surprisingly successful 'I-need-to-be-first' son strategy.

Satisfied and keen to get one up on his sibling, Sensible Son runs for a red bike.

'My bike drives faster than your bike . . . Mummy said so!' he announces to his younger brother.

Binary Boy looks to me for confirmation of this distressing fact. His face begins to crumple.

Give me strength.

God-sent granny saves the day, takes smaller sibling by the hand and leads him expertly to the jigsaws. I throw her a smile of gratitude and jog, just a touch less enthusiastically, back into the hall.

Ten minutes later, we are doing star jumps, arms and legs spread gloriously wide. Or rather, the other Body Beautifuls are. I am not. I'm bobbing about just above floor level, arms flailing wildly and legs clamped ever more firmly together with each bladder-busting bounce. I make a mental note to look for, and then look after, my elusive pelvic floor just as soon as I get home.

'Mum. MUM!' hisses another gorgeous granny, beckoning me over. I weave my way through the sweating sirens towards her.

'I think your son may have filled his nappy. I'm sorry, but you need to come. I'm afraid it's health . . .'

'And safety!' I finish for her. The impact of the inappropriately dubbed 'Nanny State' on me and my boys is becoming irritatingly apparent. Nannies were there to make life easier, weren't they? To help? Didn't the government realise I was trying to be a model mother, to make my childbirth-ravaged Body Beautiful?

'Of course,' I say, heading for the exit – again.

Wiping the sweat from my now furrowed brow, I have one of my increasingly regular maternal premonitions.

'Which one needs changing?' I ask.

'It's your eldest, I think. That one, over there . . .' She points towards Sensible Son who is sipping juice and munching his way through a pile of Rich Teas.

'But . . . but – he's not wearing a nappy . . .'

Oh well, I've done quite enough star jumps for one day.

Thankfully, I make it back from the loo in time to join in with the last few moments of toning of tums.

Working your stomach muscles assumes that you have any; and I did, in those long-forgotten days when you could have a bath without sitting on Spiderman and you could see a postman without thinking of Pat. My recent series of fortunate events has, however, endowed me with a belly which looks much less like a six-pack than a pack of wet wipes.

Five agonising crunches in and yet another granny appears at the door, an obviously famished Feisty Fellow in her helpless arms.

'I've tried rocking him, but I think he's hungry, Mum. I'm so sorry to have to drag you away from your break.'

Are you? I'm not! I rejoice silently, showering my son with grateful kisses. 'You can't help wanting a feed, can you?' I croon, sinking gratefully into a chair. He snuggles against my still jelly belly, grabs a fistful of flesh and starts to suck.

Glowing contentedly, I reflect that maybe – on this occasion – the FOB might be right. 'Nine months out, nine months in,' he reassures me regularly, when I gaze at and bemoan my still undulating body. So, if I take his nine months, and multiply that by three pregnancies, that makes, um . . . Well, at least another, oooh, eighteen months before I need to worry unduly about my porky proportions. Satisfied with this lady logic, I reach for one of my eldest son's half-eaten biscuits.

Shame to let good food go to *waist*.

★　★　★

'Foolproof!' I think smugly a fortnight later as I hurtle out of town. The boys are belted, peas in a pod, in the back of the car. 'Nothing, but nothing, can possibly go wrong this time!'

I glance happily in the rear-view mirror: three pairs of iden-tikit eyes gaze back, trusting and adoring, and I experience a tummy-lurching maternal moment. Aaahhh . . . my babies, my boys. Seized by an inexplicable sense of elation, I crank up 'Old MacDonald' and, karaoke queen, bounce along to the beat.

A sharp flash brings me back from ducks and donkeys to the reality that is the motorway on a busy Monday morning. I check the speedometer. Damn. Seventy-five in a seventy. Was that flash for me or for some other mad motorist, carried away by a rocking rhyme and an unusually sunny day? I ponder whether infant-induced insanity would stand up as an excuse for speeding in a court of law and begin composing my letter of justification in my head.

'Mummy, come on . . . sing!' commands Sensible Son from the rear.

I sigh, and then join in with gusto. At any rate, the damage – if any – has already been done.

We arrive without further mishap. 'Krazee Kingdom – Fun for all the Familee' yells the neon sign on the front of the brick building. Great, I think, corralling my offspring towards the entrance. Krazee Kingdom, here we come.

It's the smell that hits me first. Part Dettol, part pee, it takes me abruptly and none too pleasantly back to the glacial outside toilets of my Scottish primary school. I gulp, holding my breath. Hard on its odorous heels, I am assaulted next by the noise: a mixture of demented beast and savage scream. I'm convinced that the decibels are bouncing painfully off the four walls and straight into my eardrums. I plug my right ear with my one free hand, hoist the baby on to my hip, and head, a fraction less eagerly now, for the ticket desk.

Fifteen minutes later, however, I understand why parents everywhere subject themselves to the chaotic confines of the likes of Krazee Kingdom. The elder boys have disappeared into the spaghetti structure. I cannot see them, but no news, I assume, can only be good. Feisty Fellow, meanwhile, is now snoring in his car seat. I look at him disbelievingly and make a mental note that he is obviously not the 'light' sleeper we had hitherto excused. Meatloaf not Mozart at bedtime from now on. And, having put Body Beautiful on happy hold, I have treated myself to both cappuccino *and* croissant, and am luxuriating in sipping in silence and eating on my own.

At this rate, I think, casting an envious glance at the newspaper-reading mother to my left, I might even bring a book next time.

Unfortunately, the table is laminate, and although I'm not normally superstitious, I really should have touched wood.

Sensible Son screeches to a halt against my chair, splattering my knee with unusually scalding liquid.

'Mummy . . .' he pants, 'you gotta come . . . quick.' He catches sight of my crafty croissant. 'What you eatin'?' he asks suspiciously.

'Never mind that,' I deflect, hiding my illicit snack under a napkin. 'What's the matter? What's happened?'

'It's Binary Boy. He's stuck in the rope! He's at the top and he can't get down!' He gestures dramatically towards the apex of spaghetti mountain, where his younger brother is apparently incarcerated. 'He's cryin'!'

I put my cup down, ruefully accepting that the idea of hot coffee is too good to be true, and rapidly assess the situation. Feisty Fellow is asleep, but I cannot leave him. Binary Boy is stuck and needs my help. Sensible Son, strong of will and arm though he is, cannot possibly drag his slighter sibling down four floors of 'familee

68

fun'. I have, it appears, no choice. Like a decidedly less fighting-fit and female version of James Bond, I'm going in.

Murmuring apologies, I sling my miraculously still-sleeping son over one shoulder and head for the unappetising black hole.

Soft-play structures, like their shopping trolley forebears, were not designed with me in mind. I eye the tightly packed roller rods that guard the entrance with sceptical realism. Perhaps if I'd 'toned that tum' instead of eating that bun I would have stood a chance of slipping effortlessly through that gap – intended, I presume, for tiny tots or their diet-diva mums. As it stands, there is (excuse the pun) fat chance of me, my baby *and* my bottom squidging ourselves through with derrière, let alone dignity, intact, to rush to the aid of my presumably now terrified toddler.

Above the primal noises, I can, however, make out a plaintive cry emanating from the furthermost regions of the dreaded den.

'Mumma!' wails Binary Boy desperately. 'Mumma!'

That does it. Gathering babe to breast, I charge towards the roller rods, daring them to stand between me and my boy. Huffing and heaving, I gloop through, my stress-ball stomach following on politely once the remaining bony bits of my anatomy have made it safely through to the other side. I pause to catch my breath, momentarily thankful for my adaptable abs, before realising that this battle is far from won. I have merely reached base camp. The summit is still a long way off. Flexing my forearms, I grab hold of the rope and hoist myself and my baby, onwards and up . . .

Round about level two and a half, the baby has finally had enough of being force-fed through tunnels and decides to wake up. His indignant wails drown out even the wildest of whoops and I smile awkwardly and apologetically at other intrepid (and admittedly slimmer) parents who, like me, have ventured into the dome of doom.

'Gotta . . . fetch . . . middle son!' I wheeze, rolling my eyes upwards. 'He's stuck . . . at the top.' They nod silently with – I'd like to think – compassion, but I fear it could well be disapproving disdain. Undaunted, however, I soldier on.

What feels like an eternity later, we emerge, baby screaming, me sweating, into the open space that is 'The Top'. Binary Boy is sitting, cross-legged, on the padded matting next to a rope cargo net. He spots us, grins wildly and comes towards me at a run.

He is, apparently, blatantly and a touch exasperatingly, *not* stuck.

'Hello, Mumma! Look me!' he whoops joyously, before launching himself – entirely unaware of the horrors and humiliation I have endured to rescue him, my darling in distress – into the gaping mouth of a long red slide. I listen incredulously as his happy hollering gets fainter and fainter, before resuming on the outside, presumably at the very bottom.

'Come, Mumma,' he's shrieking up the interminable tube, 'you come!'

For the second time that day, I consider my legal footing. *'Absolutely NO Adults (health & safety)'* warns the wonky sign at one side of the slide. The alternative, however, for getting down that which we have only just succeeded in agonisingly ascending, is fairly unpalatable and, frankly, impossible.

'What the hell!' I yodel, throwing babe and Body Beautiful into the void. 'Watch out down there . . . we're coming through!'

My boddler boys applaud raucously as we thud to an unceremonious halt at the disapproving feet of the spaghetti structure supervisor. He glares at me in a Mr Gruber fashion, tuts loudly and stalks away.

'I think we'd better make a move, boys,' I whisper, gathering car seat and coats, before scuttling towards the suddenly appetising exit. Outside, I heave a sigh of relief, grateful to have escaped whatever punishment Krazee Kingdom dishes out these days for miscreant mothers.

The DVLA is, infuriatingly – but entirely unsurprisingly – less understanding.

As I sign the cheque and put it in the post, it occurs to me that it may have been cheaper (if not nearly as much fun) to have put my litter of lads into a kindergarten kennels.

So, How Does She Do It?
Top ten tips for surviving on Planet MOB

- Never buy the same colour socks in different sizes. Alternate.
- Surround yourself with MOBs even madder than you.
- Borrow a dog and go to puppy-training classes. Implement their top tips on your offspring just as soon as you get home.
- Never leave any job half done. If you do, someone will undo what you did do, before you come back to finish it off.
- Bake.
- Always have a ready supply of wet wipes in your bag. Long after they appear to be of little or no use.
- Beat 'em at their own game: learn to burp the alphabet backwards.
- Invest in some really good ever-clean jeans. Oh, and a pair of wellies.
- Stockpile cereal.
- Know just enough about dinosaurs to convince them you care.

Places best avoided by a Mother and her Boys

- The chocolate aisle
- Any pub with a sign up saying, '*Meals are cooked from scratch – you may have to wait*'
- A glass factory
- The London Eye with a potty-training lad★
- Great-grannies' sitting rooms full of tantalising trinkets
- All public areas where there's a risk of dog poo
- Each and every shop selling ladies' lingerie
- Any winter beach where your shivering concession is, 'OK, you may play *by* the waves, but just *don't* get wet!'
- The quiet coach on a commuter train
- A doctor's appointment involving 'womanly bits'

★*Although I have it on good authority that this is infinitely preferable to being stuck inside a capsule with a 'wailing-for-a-wee' girl: the swift downing of a bottle of Evian results in a receptacle entirely appropriate for a barely visible boy pee.*

Man-made MOB?

'De zing ish . . .' slurs my somewhat intoxicated Perfect Pair friend one Sunday afternoon in early July. 'Ze zing ish,' she begins again, concentrating hard on every word and pointing her unruly finger in the vicinity of my head, 'muvvas of boys gen'raly do . . . hic . . . end up . . . hic . . . looking liksh boys themshelfs!' she concludes triumphantly, awaiting my response with wine-tainted breath. We are standing next to a red, white and blue cheesecake at an outdoor Independence Day party. It is windy and it is cold.

Feeling a bit like an amoeba under a microscope, I look down at my paint-splattered, no-point-in-changing jeans and seen-better-days fleece with unusual interest. In a vague nod towards preparing for a party, I have swapped my winter wellies for my summer sandals, a decision that I am – given the Arctic winds – already beginning to regret. As my naked toes take on a bluish tinge, I realise that I don't have a goose-pimpled leg to stand on.

Her thesis, she expands, is based on her observations at the school gate.

The MOG arrives groomed and gleaming, long hair flowing on to impossibly high heels. Pristine white trousers and tight pink tops. Manicured nails to match her immaculate motor. White teeth dazzling, she greets her daughter with a lipstick kiss, before bobbing off calmly, and quietly, to ballet.

A MOB pick-up is, in her experience, decidedly different. Traditionally late, the MOB whirls into the playground, scattering mud from the treads of her trainers. Sporting a sensible sweatshirt and stay-clean jeans, she takes up her stance, ready to do battle with her incoming brood. One by one, her boys emerge. 'Have you got 'ny food?' they grunt as she moves in swiftly for a covert kiss. She thrusts her stand-by snack at them with nappy-gnarled hands, before corralling them quickly into the car.

'Hmmm,' I say in my stereotype-phobic, sometimes sit-on-fence fashion. I run through my memory bank of mothers, mentally checking each one against this amateur exercise in people profiling. Ignoring a few exceptional anomalies in my inexpert graph, I have to admit that she possibly has a point.

I tried wearing a skirt once.

'Enough,' I decree one morning. 'Enough of practical trousers, sensible shoes. I am a woman and today I want to look like one. Today, I'm wearing a skirt.'

Perching on the side of the bed, I wriggle myself into my one remaining pair of respectable tights and struggle into a skirt. Battling only slightly with pre-pregnancy poppers, I add a shirt and (hopefully) trendy top. Having blown the dust from the nozzle of my mostly decorative hairdryer, I carefully coif my less-than-obedient bob, before skidding, tight-toed, down the stairs. I pull on my barely-out-of-their-box knee-high boots and stand mid-kitchen, feeling ridiculously pleased with, and proud of, my female self.

'Wow, look at you!' says the FOB. 'You look lovely. Your hair – it's gorgeous!'

'Thanks,' I preen happily, 'do you like it?' Compliments are fairly rare from my pragmatic partner, so it's worth making the most of each and every one.

'Yes, I do,' he says thoughtfully, kissing me on the cheek

before heading for the door. 'You look lovely . . . all rough and ready! Like you've been dragged through a hedge backwards.'

His back burns with the intensity of my glare, but he disappears, oblivious, down the path towards the car. 'Are you going somewhere special?' he throws over his uniformed shoulder. Without waiting for a response to his apparently rhetorical question, he sets off for the relative safety of the M3 commute.

Somewhere special? As if. 'Come on, boys. Coats on, shoes on . . . we're going to be late!'

'Oooh, Mummy, what is those?' asks Feisty Fellow seconds later. He stops struggling momentarily with his dysfunctional coat zip and eyes my nearby legs with utter amazement. He moves in closer to get a better look. 'Is those your legs?'

'Of course they're my legs!' I snap in the furious wake of his damning-with-faint-praise dad. 'For goodness sake, you've seen my legs before, haven't you?'

Feisty Fellow considers this for a moment, before shaking his head. 'Only at the swimming pool. Not like this!'

Binary Boy adds to the audience. 'Your legs are so soft!' he says, salaciously stroking my unusually exposed extremities. 'What's that?' he says, stopping abruptly as he encounters a rash of stubble which has evidently found its way through my too-thin tights.

'Look, will you leave me alone, boys,' – I gently remove his inquisitive fingers – 'and put your shoes on, please . . . we *need* to get to school.'

Sensible Son eyes my attire suspiciously and comes in for the kill. 'Have you got a "meeting", Mum?' he asks.

I should explain. A 'meeting' is the term the FOB and I have adopted for any activity which means that we may well deviate from our usual predictable routine. A meeting is 'very important' and can therefore be used to excuse being late home from work, absent from an assembly or even, entirely unacceptably in the opinion of our offspring, employing the services of a babysitter and going out – *without* (how could we?) the kids.

Therefore . . . 'Mum,' he persists, 'are you going somewhere? Is that why you look so . . . so . . . strange?'

I've had enough male interest for one day.

'No, I haven't got a meeting and no, I'm not going out, am I? It's Thursday, so I'm looking after Feisty Fellow and Best Boy Friend, aren't I? We'll be at home all . . . day . . . long. This is called a SKIRT and I am wearing it because . . .'

I stop, lost. What had motivated me to put on this girly garb today, anyway? 'Because I want to. That's why. Is that OK with all of you? Any further questions? No? Good.'

Stunned by my over-emotional outburst, the boys give my legs one last lingering look, before finally, *finally* shovelling their feet into their shoes and clumping down the well-trodden road to school.

Later that morning, I've wiped up the Weetabix, put on a white wash and hung out a dark. I've finished with breakfast, laid up for lunch and even started on supper. My youngest son and his friend are busy being pirates upstairs. So I sit down at the computer in the study for a furtive Facebook fix.

'What's on your mind?' asks the innocuous headline. I scan the page for interesting insights into other people's lives.

'Just been handed my new Jimmy Choos by a *gorgeous* delivery man. Isn't it wonderful getting packages in the post?' mews Manicured MOG. I try to think of the last item *I* had delivered to *my* door. An industrial screwdriver, if I'm not mistaken, so that the FOB can finally mend the dodgy study door handle that has been broken for, oooh, as long as I can remember. Fixing door handles is, the FOB explains as he heads into the garden, a winter job. Joyous. Only a few more months then of living in fear of being stuck in the study – me on the inside, the knob on the out.

Anyway, I think, turning my attention back to the screen and reflecting on my own exceptionally unexciting retail experience, my screwdriver delivery man was more gobstopper than eye candy. I sigh deeply at the unfairness of it all.

'Hello, boys. What are you up to?' I jump guiltily, as if they've caught me pinching from their party bags, as they clatter down the stairs and race into the room. Feisty Fellow grabs hold of the handle and slams the door forcefully shut behind him.

It closes with an innocent, unassuming click.

Like a too-predictable murder scene in a low-budget film, my world slows scarily down. Face full of fear, I rise from the chair, arms outstretched before me, and moonwalk towards the now impenetrable wall of wood. But I know already that I'm much too late. 'Nooooo!' I mouth. 'Noooooo.'

Then – silence.

The boys look at me. I look at the boys. I look at the door. I put my head in my hands.

'What's wrong, Mummy?' asks Feisty Fellow.

I turn to face him. Try to compose myself. 'It's OK, it's fine. It's just that the study door is a teeny-weeny bit *shut* and as the handle is just a teeny-weeny bit *broken*, it means that we are just possibly, maybe . . . absolutely . . . *stuck*.' Other words spring to mind, but I hold my tongue.

He gazes at me blankly, just a teeny bit 'not bovvered'.

'Oh dear,' he says happily. He and Best Boy Friend pull a game off the shelf and settle down peacefully, to play on the carpet.

Right, I think, assuming an air of practical competence I

certainly don't feel. Right. The phone's in the sitting room on the other side of the door, so I can't phone a friend. Our nearest neighbour is elderly and will never hear my cries for help. And anyway, I've bolted the back door on the inside as I always do when I'm home alone, so even if I can attract someone's attention, they won't be able to get in to the house to free us from our impromptu prison. As the minutes pass, I start to get ever so slightly – to use one of Sensible Son's more eloquent adjectives – 'freaked'.

Then suddenly I remember: the key, the spare key to the patio doors. Down the road with our second-nearest neighbours. If they are in, and if they can find it, I can get into the kitchen via the patio and it will all be over. *If.*

First things first though – I have to get out of the study.

I eye the one available escape route. The study window is rather high – too high to hoist out even the most biddable of boys, but . . . I crane my head . . . if I teeter on the table and clamber out on to the window ledge, I can probably, possibly – just about – leap down and out and into the garden below. It might not work, but I have two tots, no food, no loo and no plan B. It's worth a try.

In a move more befitting Karate Kid than the lady I am attempting, that day, to be, I jerk my left leg up on to the table. My too-tight skirt gives an agitated rip.

'Dammit,' I curse, as I lurch my right one up to join its partner. I can feel the skirt seam beginning to unravel, travelling rapidly up the back of my overstretched tights. 'Great. Just great,' I grumble, wondering what on earth had possessed me – even temporarily – to try to masquerade as a MOG.

Instructing the mercifully unaware boys to 'stay there' and that I'll be 'right back', I open the window as wide as its hinges allow, grab on to the frame and prepare to launch myself on to the lawn. Once I'm out, I realise, looking fearfully down, there can be no going back.

With NASA precision, I prepare for blast-off. At the critical moment, however, I suffer a slight, but significant, last-minute glitch. Skidding on the sill, I fail to leap safely out and *over* the bush which buffets the study window, and instead, find myself propelled, feet first, into its thorny folds.

'Dammit . . . and then some!' I curse again, slightly louder this time, pulling my painfully laddered legs out of the innards of the bush, and back on to relatively safe garden ground. Checking that the boys are still otherwise occupied, I dash down the track in search of salvation and The Key.

'Need . . . spare . . . key . . . now!' I gasp at my amazingly unperturbed neighbour, as he opens his door to my frantic knocks. Ignoring my homespun fishnet stockings, he scrabbles in a drawer in a table in his hall.

'This one yours?' I nod, grab the key and race back whence I came.

Half an hour later, my palpitations have started to subside and the blood on my legs has begun to dry. The damage to my tights is, however, irrevocable. Heavy of heart and admitting defeat, I take off my skirt, dig my jeans out of the wash basket and slip them on like the second skin they have, perhaps predictably, become. Pulling on a pair of worn woolly socks, I clump, transformed, back down to the boys.

Feisty Fellow looks up from his emergency egg and soldiers. 'You look bootiful, Mummy,' he declares earnestly, yolk dribbling down his chin.

'Oh . . . thank you,' I say, both pleased and surprised. I add my skirt to the ever-hopeful mending mound and stuff my too-torn tights in the bin.

Sometimes, I think, you have to go round – and round – the houses to end up back where you began.

When I was seven, I wrote to Father Christmas.

'Pleez can I have a princess dress in my stocking?'

To my eternal disappointment, the garment never appeared. Because despite the fact that I spent most of my childhood days in the wilds of the Scottish woods with my farmer's-daughter friends, making moss soap and bracken beds, despite my mainly unisex attire, I do remember wishing, every now and then, that I could look like – if not be – a 'girly girl'.

A picture of me at my ninth birthday party shows me with a beaming smile, brandishing an extremely unflattering, but surely stylish, horizontally striped skirt and a batwing bee jumper in blinding shades of black and yellow. Essential additions to any woman's wardrobe.

A later photo shows a peroxide perm – the result of my first ever haircut that did not involve my mother, a pair of kitchen scissors and a large Pyrex bowl. With hindsight, the bowl was probably preferable to the perm, but at the time I loved my 'Princess of Wales' waves.

And at sixteen, I was finally allowed to pierce my ears – 'You're old enough now to make your own mistakes!' – and huge hoops dangled from my invariably infected lobes. I was in my twenties before I made the sensible switch to silver studs.

As a teenager, I discovered boys, booze and bad pop music. I cried when Charlene and Scott walked up the aisle (why her, not me and look at that dress!); I danced long and slow as a Lady in Red; I spent my monthly allowance on leg warmers and lace.

At university, I joined every club under the sun and attended only one, I learned about languages and love, about loneliness and Lycra. I did aerobics and alcohol, circuits and cakes. I was neither glamorous girl, nor totally tomboy. I enjoyed a bit of everything, took the blue with the pink; I looked, to all intents and purposes, like absolutely average Annie.

And then I met the FOB. And then I became MOB.

With the advent of each bundle of boy, have I morphed from average Annie to in-transit Toni to now fully fledged Fred? Have I progressed from 'fe-male' to 'she-male' to now entirely 'man-made MOB'? Might Perfect Pair's theory that mothers of boys tend to look more male themselves be more than just an alcohol-fuelled assertion?

I look around my bedroom. My clothes are practical: black, brown or blue. I own three pairs of shoes: summer sandals (this year's version of last year's – brown), winter boots (ditto) and the inevitable and aforementioned wellington boots (actually green, but mostly caked in mud, so that colour and make are utterly irrelevant). My make-up (expensive) was bought for my wedding, my hairspray (full) smells suspiciously like wine. Even my sensible studs languish under layers of dressing-table dust.

I bought a pair of *pink* slippers once for the sheer hell of it. They flash like a lighthouse in my ocean of blue.

But would my wardrobe have looked any different had I been tickled pink, rather than blessed with blue? Would I have worn more foundation, more lipstick, more mascara, if I had a glitter of girls, rather than my battalion of boys? Would my 'me' have been more 'she', if I knew the patter of female feet, rather than the barrage of boy boots?

I have to admit that I don't know. So I put my premenstrual musings to the FOB.

'Do you think I look like a boy?' I ask him one morning, scrutinising myself in our one full-length mirror.

'Not at all,' he shouts from the kitchen. 'You're far too . . . er . . . what's the word?' He's obviously struggling. 'Curvy – yes, that's it. You've far too many curves to be a boy!' He sounds pleased to have done his duty, relieved.

I eye my 'curves' with reluctant resignation. 'No, not my body itself. My clothes – how I look . . .'

'I think you look fine,' he says, as I walk into the kitchen. He even glances up from whatever it is he is doing. 'Better than fine – good!' he adds, hopefully.

I stare at him. 'What on earth are you doing?' He appears to be decanting my skimmed milk into the boys' carton of full-fat. And I don't like full-fat.

'Ah, yes – I just need one more milk carton for the counter-balance of the tree-house trap door, so I . . . er . . .'

I stare at him again, harder this time. 'Couldn't you just have put mine in a jug? Anyway,' I continue, aware that the calorific damage has already been done, 'I've been thinking . . . I might get myself some more feminine clothes. Maybe something floaty, something fashionable, something pink . . . I might see if Manicured MOG wants to come shopping with me!'

The mention of Manicured MOG finally ensures his un-divided attention. He can already see the pounds dropping off our bank balance like an overly eager weight watcher.

'But . . . but . . . you've always liked blue; you've never worn pink . . .' Suddenly, he looks genuinely scared at the prospect of my reincarnation as Makeover MOB with the redoubtable aid of my minted MOG friend. 'Anyway,' he adds, 'you've always said that you don't see the point of following fashion!'

'That,' I retort huffily, 'is *not* the point. Has it ever occurred to you that I might – just OCCASIONALLY – want to look like a LADY, instead of more like a man?'

Like his sons before him, he is struck silent, dumb, by my out-of-nowhere oestrogen outburst.

'But darling,' he says, when he is quite, quite sure that I've well and truly finished, 'no one's stopping you, are they?' He fills my now empty milk carton with water and heads outside to the bottom of the garden.

I never do go clothes shopping with Manicured MOG.

Instead, the FOB suggests that my Kindred MOB friend and I head off for some well-earned 'me time' together. We sit in the jacuzzi having a good girly chat. Gossip is so much more satisfying – and cheaper – than Gucci.

And so I have to concede that the FOB is probably right. How I choose to look is, after all, down to me – no one else. I am who *I* am, I wear what *I* want. Boys or no boys, I don't think that I would ever have had a natural propensity to be overly and outrageously pretty in pink.

While I may occasionally enjoy flashing my plumage like the ironically male peacock, I am fundamentally happiest in brown, blending in, in black. Ultimately, despite sporadic flirtations with femininity or dalliances with dresses, I am, and probably always have been, more of a 'he' than a 'she' in the world of the wardrobe. And whether the abundance of sons and my boy-biased life have merely allowed me to manifest my existing true-blue tendencies more appropriately, more extensively, I will, obviously, never know.

I catch up with the now sober Perfect Pair on the phone.

'I've been thinking about what you said at that party. You know, about mothers of boys looking more male?' There's silence on the line; I can sense that she's searching her post punch-drunk brain. 'Chicken ... or egg,' I say meaningfully, 'chicken, or egg?'

She clucks like a bemused bantam, and hangs up the phone.

Clothes conundrums and soul searching over (for the time being at least), I don my filthy wellies and faithful jeans and set off along the lanes after the lads in my life.

The wind blows my too-long locks across my make-up-free face and I smile through the thatch, knowing that this is the woman my FOB fell in love with, that this is the look which he still likes best, that this is *my* look.

We climb the hill, skirt the edge of a field. Stop at a small clump of trees.

It appears that neither Feisty Fellow nor I went to the loo before we set off. Despite repeated reminders, he 'forgot' while, in the interests of getting out sometime before supper, I 'forsook'.

'Poor Mummy,' says Feisty Fellow, adopting the position in front of the first convenient conifer. 'You hasn't got a willy like us, has you? You needs to sit down to wee from your bottom!'

'Hmmm,' I say vaguely, not wishing to embark on a lesson in female physiology right here, right now. I jiggle up and down, considering my options.

The FOB leaps to the rescue.

'Do you need the loo?' he asks enthusiastically before delving deep into his Scooby snack rucksack. 'I knew this would come in handy one day!'

I look at the object he is thrusting towards me: a plastic funnel, shaped suspiciously like a mini-male member. 'You must have left it in the bag after our mountain marathon, remember?'

I nod. I do remember: 'A Shewee,' my fellow female team-mate had chortled, handing me my unlikely pre-challenge present. 'It's the ultimate accessory for when we're "caught short" up top! If we can't beat the boys, at least now we can join 'em!' Visions of communal pee-stops had swum unappetisingly in front of my Karrimor-clad eyes and I'd smiled a tepid thanks. Unsurprisingly, I'd never been sufficiently desperate to make use of the plastic penis, and so the Shewee had returned, unused, in its box. Thereafter, it had disappeared from my sight and my mind. Until now.

I eye the proffered prosthetic, thank my spouse for his kind concern . . . and begin my long trek back home, alone, to the loo.

I may be a ewe in mostly ram's clothing and I may be mostly happy as such, but the Shewee would push this honorary She-he just one stiletto step too far.

You know you're a MOB when you have some (or all) of these in the back pocket of your jeans:

- A piece of Lego
- A Pokemon card
- A shell
- A conker
- A snotty tissue
- A marble, or three
- Crumbled breadsticks
- One sock
- A plaster (new)
- A plaster (used)

A MOB's Wardrobe

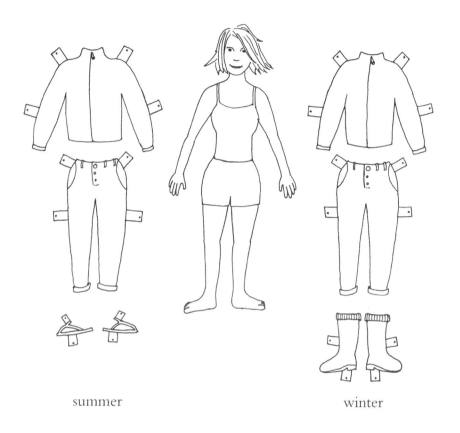

summer   winter

Definition of a sweater:
An item of clothing worn by a son when his mother is chilly

It's never plane sailing with boys on board

It seemed like a good idea at the time.

'I've got summer leave coming up,' said the FOB scanning his ever-present diary one sunny Sunday evening. 'We could get away for our first holiday "in famille", as it were. Where do you fancy going? A few days in Cornwall? A week in Wales? Obviously,' he gestured towards the Moses basket where his firstborn son lay, arms above head like a surrendering soldier, 'we can't do anything *too* mad this year.'

I thought for a moment. 'Let's,' I said, inspired presumably by his gallant attempt at franglais and the complete lack of grip on reality which accompanies giving birth, 'let's go to France!' I beamed at him enthusiastically.

'France?' he replied, struck dumb or dumbstruck, I've never known which. Either way, in this instance, both were equally appropriate.

'Yes, France. We could rent a gîte somewhere down south for a week, somewhere warmer than the UK. Just think . . . the cafés, the croissants . . . a leetle vin rouge? It'd be good to get away and Sensible Son'd love the change of scene!'

He stared at me, trying to decide whether I was pulling one of his long legs, or whether I had, in fact, gone stark-raving mother mad. He decided on the latter.

'You're serious, aren't you? You really want to go all the way to France with an eight-week-old baby?'

I might have been suggesting a safari in the savannah for all the enthusiasm my idea was eliciting.

'Why not? We can take the car, catch a ferry from Portsmouth. You're always saying what a great traveller Sensible Son is when we drive down to Devon – the moment the revs go above 3600 he's out for the count!'

Sensible Son snuffled sweetly; his basket creaked.

'But Devon's only three hours away, not a 600km slog in a different time zone!' the FOB pointed out. Even he, however, knew better than to argue with a post-natal mum on a mission. 'OK, OK,' he acquiesced. 'France it is . . . we'll give it a go.'

To be fair, we make it past Paris without too much ado.

By this time, it's late morning. We have been up since – even for those accustomed to early starts – some heathenly horrendous hour, and despite several espressos as we traversed the Channel, my husband and I are feeling decidedly jaded. My eyes struggle to stay open to read the map, the FOB stifles a yawn with steering-wheel-stiff hands. At this moment in time, it all seems a lot of extra effort for a bona fide baguette.

Our son, on the other hand, comatose to Le Mans, has apparently done all the sleeping he's about to do.

He announces his awakening as only an infant knows how.

'Waaaaaaaahhhhhhhh!' he declares. 'Waaaaaaaaaahhhhhhhh!'

I smile hopefully at the FOB.

'He'll drift back off again in a minute like he always does. He's just saying hello,' I say. His ongoing wails suggest that greeting his parents is not the aim of his game.

Ten minutes further on down the autoroute his protests show little signs of abating.

'I'll stop at the next aire,' shouts his father over the screams.

'He's probably just hungry,' I shout back, glancing at the clock. Shouldn't be though, I think, not if we're going by 'The Book'. 'Probably all that sea air on the boat!' I suggest pseudo-brightly. My lack-of-sleep drunken sailor acknowledges me with a grunt.

Some time later we're back en route. Baby fed, bladders emptied, all good. The FOB starts the engine. The baby opens his mouth.

'Waaaaaaahhhhhh!' he declares again. 'Waaaaaaaahhhhh-hhhh!'

The FOB looks at me, eyebrows ever so slightly raised.

'He's probably just tired now . . . he'll be asleep in a sec.'

The eyebrows rise ever so slightly higher.

As, unfortunately, do the noise levels.

I consult the map. 'There's another aire in 20km,' I say meekly.

My 'whose-idea-was-this-anyway-but-I'm-too-tired-to-argue' husband sighs, puts his foot down and overtakes a 2CV.

'Right,' I say emphatically, another half-hour and 16-euro stop later, 'he's been changed, he's been burped, he's been fed. He cannot *possibly* want anything this time.' I strap my son into his car seat and stoop to kiss his downy forehead. He gives me the most fleeting of smiles, sufficient to melt my now thoroughly depleted bosoms. I settle myself into my seat; the FOB turns the key.

As if his lungs and the ignition are umbilically interlinked, Sensible Son revs up more abruptly than the engine itself.

'Waaaaaahhhhhhh!' he declares with all-too-familiar predictability. 'Waaaaaaahhhhhhh!'

The FOB grimaces, grips the wheel and nevertheless prepares to depart.

'We'd have been in Cornwall by now,' he sighs.

'Really?' I say. Sometimes less is more.

★   ★   ★

'Well,' I burble just outside Tours, 'we were going to have to fill up *sometime* soon, anyway.' I glance hopefully at the blatantly 'half-full' fuel gauge and even more hopefully at my losing-patience partner.

'Sleep all the way, that's what you said,' he rumbles. 'And I said three hours, maybe . . . but not thirteen!' I sense his storm clouds are very gradually gathering.

'I'll just give him a little top-up while you fill the car, shall I?' I simper. At times, sticking to routine can prove counterproductive. 'Oh, and don't forget it's "sans plomb" you want . . .' I remind him.

I can't quite hear what he roars in reply, but I assume it's a grateful appreciation of my linguistic skills.

Still.

'There,' I soothe, as my baby boy turns his head to gaze up at me from his personal petrol pump. 'Is that better? You *are* a hungry wee man today, aren't you . . . maybe it's one of those growth spurts the manuals mention.' He blinks, puffs out his admittedly rounded cheeks. Whimpers. I sling a muslin over my shoulder, prop him up against it, rub his back. He burps, none too quietly. 'That's bett . . . eurggghhhh!'

With an efficiency and accuracy any good painter would be proud of, Sensible Son succeeds in whitewashing the muslin, his mother, the seatbelt and beyond. I sit, stunned and splattered, unsure of quite how to extricate either myself or my baby from my now sodden seat.

'Do you want anything from the shop?' asks the FOB, poking his head through the window. 'Oh,' he says, spotting my saturated state. 'Right. Ummm . . .'

'Take him, please,' I say, passing the parcel. Dripping milk and mucus, I clamber from the car.

Looking back on this episode with the benefit of years, and

not weeks, since the desensitising exposures of childbirth and with more of a sleep-sustained grip on reality, I would not do now what I did next. But at the time, exhausted and, well, wet, it felt like a perfectly natural thing to do.

So, in the middle of a French petrol station, in the middle of the day, I strip off. Take off my top, struggle out of my trousers and stand by the sans-plomb pump in my less than stylish nursing bra and pants.

More aware of the astonishment and outrage of numerous Poirot lookalikes than his apparently oblivious semi-starkers wife, the FOB quickly delves into the boot and throws me some clothes. I pull on a tracksuit and climb back into the car. While my impromptu striptease may have taken mere moments, I suspect it has a longer-lasting impact on the unfortunate audience. They speed off in their Citroëns, armed, no doubt, with fresh ammunition about the eccentricity of the English.

Around about Poitiers, we finally admit defeat. We pull in to an unappetising ring-road motel and check in for the night.

'Apparently,' says the FOB, now verging on the delirious, 'they're having a heatwave in Wales.'

'Right . . .' I murmur apologetically and hurry inside.

We manage just four unseasonally frigid days in the south of France before, with three overnight stops pre-booked en route, we embark on the laborious limp back home.

OK.

So cars aren't the best way to travel with tots. But taking to the skies? That must surely be faster, with less potential for puke.

Thus.

'We gonna see Daddy,' lisps Sensible Son.

'How nice,' says the lady at check-in. 'How many bags?'

'Daddy's ship's at sea,' he tries again.

'Really?' says the airport android, with an astonishing lack of interest. 'Passports . . .'

'We goin' to Malta . . . to meet Daddy!' he chants gleefully.

His smaller sibling grins in enthusiastic accord. 'Dadda! Dadda!' shrieks Binary Boy from his buggy, frantically searching for his favourite FOB. His father, who, unfortunately for him and the rest of Gatwick's North Terminal, is way out of earshot, serving on a frigate, mid-Mediterranean.

'Gate sixty-five, boarding twelve forty-five,' drones the clone, doing an impressive impression of one who couldn't care less.

'Thank you,' I say, trying to make eye contact and maybe elicit some emotion. Failing. 'Oh,' I gabble over my shoulder as we prepare to leave her to her gloom, 'we have got priority boarding, haven't we?'

'You'd have paid when you booked. Next!' Summarily dismissed, I grab the buggy, bags and boy and speed on my way.

Fearing that the trek from check-in to gate could involve an unexpected tour of *all* of North Terminal's tunnels, I route march my hot-to-trot toddler and his buggy-bound brother swiftly past the attractions of cafés and Dunkin' Donuts. Down countless corridors, up endless escalators. We arrive at gate sixty-five as instructed, a little sweaty, but with half an hour to spare. My eldest collapses in a chair as I scan the board.

'Can't see the Malta flight listed . . .' I mutter. 'Maybe we're too early . . . they'll probably put it up in a minute.' I sink gratefully into a seat and plop Sensible Son on my lap. We get out Hungry Caterpillar and dutifully debate its diet.

Ten minutes later, I glance at the board again. Mallorca, Amsterdam, but still no Malta.

'Excuse me,' I ask a gratifyingly more approachable airline employee, 'is the Malta flight delayed?'

She consults her computer. 'Malta . . . Malta . . . no, it's on time, madam. Twelve forty-five, gate sixty-six.'

Sixty-six? 'But . . . but I was told gate sixty-five.'

She shakes her head. 'No, it's definitely sixty-six.'

'So,' I say, a note of panic creeping into my voice, 'where *is* gate sixty-six?'

Now, as anyone who has had the dubious delight of discovering knows, it does not *necessarily* follow that the whereabouts of gate sixty-six bears any kind of physical proximity to that of gate sixty-five. Indeed, I have a sneaking suspicion that somewhere, out there, an airport planner takes sadistic delight in watching the horrified faces of hapless travellers like myself, who realise – too late – that they are indeed at the wrong gate and that getting to the right one could take some time.

Time which today I haven't got.

I grab my baggage, human and otherwise, and hurtle from the gate back the way we came.

They are announcing priority boarding as we career around the corner.

Thank goodness I paid the extra for that, I think, as I eye the bulging departure lounge. It is packed to the brim with now upstanding tourists, armed with carry-on luggage and the wild look of those who are desperate to depart. The idea of having to jostle in line for half an hour with two tired children and excess baggage doesn't fill me or, I would hazard a guess, my fellow passengers, with unadulterated elation.

Somewhat self-consciously and apologetically, I manoeuvre myself and my sons towards the front of the queue.

'Sorry,' I say as I threaten to amputate the toes of a fellow traveller with my over-burdened buggy, 'but we have priority boarding.'

He regards us dispassionately; I think he may well have been separated from airport android at birth. 'So do I,' he says. 'And so do they . . .' – he gestures towards the line which snakes all the way from passports to the back of beyond.

I stare at the 80 per cent of travellers who have apparently paid for the 'luxury' of early-bird boarding. Blink back the tears. And, not for the first time today, I put boys and buggy in reverse.

Some not insubstantial time later, we finally board the plane. Sensible Son is strapped in to his window seat, beautifully distracted by the up and down motion of the plastic sun shade. Binary Boy is strapped to my lap with a device even less straightforward than Gatwick's gate-numbering system. I breathe out and relax for the first time today.

I've made it to the plane, in time and intact, and in a matter of hours we will be reunited – for a short time, at least – with the boys' beloved dad. I allow myself to savour, for a moment, our imagined meeting.

The plane jolts alive and we taxi slowly out to the runway.

We are still climbing steeply skywards when Sensible Son grabs my elbow.

'Wee wee coming,' he whispers.

Now?

'I asked you if you needed one before we boarded,' I tell him as if this makes a blind bit of difference to a two-year-old's bladder. 'You said you didn't need one!'

He stares at me blankly with his big blue eyes.

'Wee wee coming!' he reiterates.

'Can you just hang on a minute . . . just a minute . . .' I stare hopefully at the 'Fasten seatbelt' sign, willing it to switch off. The light remains unobligingly on. 'Think about something else,' I suggest. 'I know . . . Hungry Caterpillar's chocolate cake!'

Sensible Son moans delightedly and shifts in his seat.

'S'OK, Mummy,' he says, 'wee wee's gone.'

Thank goodness for that, I think, blessing the distracting powers of both Eric Carle and chocolate. Any moment now the sign will switch off and we'll be free to go pee.

'S' gone,' he announces proudly, 'cos I's dun it!'

I examine the nether regions of my smiling son. What once was his seat is now a steaming pool of pee. While he may be relieved, I most certainly am not.

Quickly, I reach for the call button to hail a hostess. She passes me a cloth with French-polished hands. 'These things happen!' she chirps with a lipgloss smile.

'Apparently so,' I say, as I begin my maternal mopping-up operation and she strides off, ever so elegantly, up the aisle.

I *know* these things undoubtedly happen, but somehow I doubt they happen to *her*.

Three hours later we touch down.

My back aches from tottering up . . . and . . . down the aisle with Binary Boy.

My bladder throbs from the sheer impossibility of cramming both me and my kids inside an airborne loo.

My head pounds from the relentless banging of that ruddy sun shade.

The FOB greets us at arrivals with a grin and a kiss.

'Good flight?' he asks, throwing Sensible Son in the air, before hugging me hard.

I look at him blankly and burst into tears.

I can't quite remember what possessed us to travel from Winchester to Aberdeen by train.

Perhaps it was the extortionate cost of five plane tickets;

perhaps it was the unenvironmental impact of taking the car. More probably, it was that the pain of previous plane and automobile excursions had still to subside. Whatever the reason, this time we were absolutely adamant we'd let the train take the strain. And third time's lucky, so they say.

'Have a good trip!' says my saintly lift-to-the-station friend, as we stagger from her car one wintery dawn. 'I don't envy you!' she chuckles, watching us pile our cases high on the pavement.

'We'll be fine . . . OK, so it *is* quite a long way, but at least on the train you're not stuck in one seat, and at least this time, I'm not travelling on my own.' She grins ambiguously, and starts to set off. Somehow, I resist the temptation to hurl our mounds of luggage at my unsuspecting husband and sprint up the road after her rapidly disappearing car.

'Hi ho!' I sing instead to my trolley-touting sons. 'It's off to London we go!' I pick up a rucksack and skip down the steps. Three dwarves and one giant follow happily behind.

The timetable for the morning goes something like this:

08:23	Clamber aboard the train to London Waterloo. Find seats and encourage boys to put behinds on to them.
08:23½	Instruct children to take feet off seats and replace shoes with bottoms.
08:25	First 'Are we nearly there yet?' (Middle son)
08:26	Re-instruct children to take feet off seats – threaten with incurring the undoubted wrath of 'The Fat Controller'.
08:29	Second 'Are we nearly there yet?' (Youngest son)
08:30	The Fat Controller arrives. Entertains children with his ticket machine. Unfortunately a very nice, and

actually thin, man. Puts paid to any potential for using him as a scary 'shoes on seats' sanction.

08:34   Third 'Are we nearly there yet?' (Eldest son, standing up on his seat and making breath bubbles on the window. Middle son leaps alongside. Youngest son wobbles to join his brothers, slips off the seat and crashes to the floor. Screams ensue.)

08:35   Fourth 'Surely we *must* be nearly there!' (Underbreath supplications from both the MOB and FOB)

And so the train trundles on and on.

By Basingstoke our boys sing to a different tune.

'I'm hungry!'

'Me too!'

'Me three!' they moan.

Train travel is a hungry business, it seems.

'Aha,' I think confidently, 'I've got this one covered.' Learning from the experience of my cheap-as-chips flight to Malta, where purchasing a sandwich cost the same as your seat, I have packed a homespun picnic fit for a prince. Or, in this instance, three bored boys and their 'still a growing lad!' dad.

Unstrapping my rucksack, I present my improbably famished family with eight Tupperware tubs full of cucumber, carrots and raisins; six bags of Teddy Bear crisps (three as emergency back-up in the event of 'leaves on the line'); three plastic-fantastic tubes of Cheestrings (not generally encouraged, but they do take days to dissect); ditto yoghurt-covered raisins (take ages to eat); two extra-large loaves'-worth of assorted sandwiches; four gallons of water and, with a final flourish, a full-to-the brim flask of cafetière coffee.

I sit back and wait for appreciation and applause.

None is forthcoming.

They fall on my picnic like coyote on a carcass.

By Woking, only the bare bones are left. My now satiated pack are finally sitting in their seats, holding their stomachs and licking their lips. 'That's it then,' I announce dispassionately, 'food finished till Aberdeen!' They gaze at me somewhat drunkenly with goody-glazed eyes. And then, as inevitably as a moany Monday follows a too-late-to-bed Sunday, the post-prandial event ensues.

09:00   First trip to the loo (Middle son)
09:02   Second trip to the loo (Eldest and youngest sons)
09:04   Third trip to the loo (Youngest son, accompanied by the MOB. Didn't get to push the button last time and is teetering on a tantrum unless allowed to take 'his turn'.)

Now as any weak-bladdered commuter can confirm, using a train toilet is far from straightforward when adults are involved. But taking a small boy to the loo while rattling along rails is probably about as bad as it gets. Actually, I take that back. Helping a girl to spend her penny 'on line' without her either contracting some dreadful disease or flooding the floor must (I can only imagine) be decidedly more difficult.

Feisty Fellow finally gets to push his all-important button and the toilet door hisses open. Grabbing his arm with one hand and pinching my nose with the other, I gingerly cross the threshold and enter the loo.

'Let's get this over and done with,' I suggest nasally. Feisty Fellow obligingly pulls down his pants and goes to automatically lift the seat.

'Don't touch that!' I shriek. While exposure to bacteria apparently helps develop children's immune systems, surely touching all-too-visible viruses really can't be clever?

Legs spread John Wayne style, he proceeds to pee.

He's mid-flow and aiming unusually accurately, when the train lurches suddenly and wildly to the left. Water and wee slosh everywhere from basin and bog, splattering all who have dared to step inside. Feisty Fellow looks down at his now urine-soaked shoes; his face puckers.

'What is it with me and uninvited excretions?' I huff, as I grab a wodge of paper towels and begin, once again, to mop up mess.

We make it to Waterloo without further incident, Womble underground across London, and emerge into the brightness of King's Cross Station.

Feeling not unlike Mrs Weasley at the start of term (only without the ginger hair and her Ginny-girl, of course) I guide my mini train travellers and trolleys across the station to the platform where, I have it on authority, our carriage awaits. I check the departures screen surreptitiously as we pass it by (you never know quite when the 'change-the-gate joker' may be watching in wait) before, satisfied, leading my troop towards our train.

I am not fazed by the hordes who have also, it appears, chosen today to chuff their way to Aberdeen. After all, our tickets are pre-booked, we have pre-assigned seats. Forward facing in two consecutive rows, coach C. This time, I'm not leaving anything to chance.

Ah, here we go, coach A . . . B . . . C . . .

'What's wrong?' asks the FOB as I halt, abruptly. The boys bumper-car up behind. 'Blimey, it's packed!' he says staring at the train.

'It's not that . . .' I tremble, motioning towards coach C. 'Look!'

His year-round tan turns scarily pale. 'Oh no!' he whispers, spying the sticker on the window. 'The boys . . . US . . . *thirteen* stops . . . *nine* hours. All the way to Aberdeen in a *Quiet* Coach?'

He laughs, a little manically. I offer up a prayer. With no alternative, we bundle the boys on board.

So to recap.

Somewhere, out there, there is a carriage-worth of commuters who are trying to get their money back on their Quiet Coach tickets.

Somewhere, out there, there is an aeroplane flying high, with seats ponging faintly of pee.

And somewhere, out there, there's me and my underwear on French CCTV.

So for them, for us and for the foreseeable, perhaps me and my boys should stick to holidays at home.

Are We Nearly There Yet?
The best travel games for Boys on board

- 'I spy' – although for reasons of sanity best to wait till they know *all* of their alphabet.
- Count the number of cars/tractors/drunks/roadkill on the road. Adapt according to location.
- 'I went shopping and I bought . . .' memory game. But only play this if you accept *you* won't win.
- Sums (addition/subtraction/multiplication . . . whatever). Can (and does) go on for ever. Warning: this is not a game to embark on when you're tired. Serious risk of falling asleep at the wheel.
- Create the longest word possible from number-plate letters. A bit like travel Scrabble. Therefore, be prepared for outraged discussion and violent debate. Never a good idea when crammed in a car.
- Alternatively, forget all the above and beg, buy or steal a travel DVD player. Believe me, give in once and you'll never look back.

The Ultimate Mother of Boys' Cross Word

[1]S	A	N	D	W	I	C	H				
Q											
U						[2]N					
[3]A	R	E	W	E	T	H	E	R	E	?	[4]M
B						A					A
B				[5]S	C	R	E	E	N		G
L						L					A
E				[6]W	H	Y		[7]B			Z
				I			[8]V	O	M	I	T
				P				R		N	
				E		[9]H		E		E	
		[10]C	R	O	S	S	W	O	R	D	S
							M				
			[11]F	I	D	G	E	T			

110

Across

1. Item purchased on train for same price as seat (8 letters, no taste)
3. The question your offspring ask as you leave the drive (3 words, 3, 2, 5 and a '?')
5. The only way to avoid 1 down (6)
6. The question you ask yourself as you leave the drive (1 word and a sigh)
8. Bound to happen at least once upon a time (5)
10. En-route entertainment; the expletives emanating from a travelling MOB's mouth (5,5)
11. What boys do best on an overcrowded plane (6)

Down

1. Oh-so-helpful boy behaviour in times of travel stress (8)
2. The MOB lie reply to 3 across (6)
4. Redundant item in MOB hand luggage (8)
6. Essential item in MOB hand luggage (5)
7. 'I'm _ _ _ _ _' says your son, only seconds after setting off (5)
9. The ideal holiday destination for MOBs (4, sad but true)

Barbie or Ben 10, gender will out

Oldest Friend comes to visit. We stand in my unusually clean kitchen, drinking unusually hot coffee, while the children play – unusually quietly.

Oldest Friend is now a MOG.

'What are those for?' she asks, eyeing the complicated-looking plastic padlocks that adorn both the fridge and freezer doors.

'Those? Oh, they're just fridge locks – keep the food in, fingers out! You've no idea how much easier life has been since we put them on.'

She eyes me with the inquisitive interest of one who has encountered a new, and not entirely sane, species.

'Is that so?' she murmurs, blatantly uncomprehending and an iota disdainful. 'Shall I make some tea? Where are your cups?'

'Thanks,' I say gratefully, sinking my pregnant-with-number-three bulk into a chair. 'Mugs? In the cupboard next to the dishwasher – over there.'

She bends to open the door; tugs and tugs again.

'I can't . . . um, I think the door's stuck!'

'Oh yeah, sorry. No – not stuck – you just need to release the catch on the inside. It's the door locks for the boys. What a great invention – you should get some!'

'Hmm,' she says, casting me a glance that is filled at once with pity and fear. She looks round at her Gorgeous Girl, engrossed in Polly Pockets at the kitchen table. I can tell that she's not entirely convinced.

Some years later, I'm trying to pair up three different sizes of identical black socks when the phone rings. Grateful for any diversion from this entirely impossible endeavour, I rush to pick it up.

'Hi, it's me,' says Oldest Friend. Twelve months before, she too joined the MOB.

'You know those padlock-type things you have on your fridge door?' she asks, almost sheepishly. I cast around blankly, trying to catch up with her train of thought. Then I remember.

'Oh yes. Those. They were great when the boys were small. I finally took them off last year when I realised that the only person unable to open them any more was me when I've food in one hand and flour on the other!'

'Yes, anyway . . .' she interrupts. Time is obviously of the essence. 'Where did you get them?'

I smile and try not to feel smug. Welcome to my world, MOB. Welcome!

Girls are *not* born the same as boys.

There. I've said it. I've come out, spoken up. No more sitting on the nature/nurture fence. It's time to jump off and put my meanderings where my mouth is, even at the risk of derision and denial.

Because I am not a psychologist. And I am not an academic. But I am a mother and I have seen more than my fair share of mini hes and mini shes to be able to claim with confidence that whether or not you (or indeed I) like it, their sex *does* play a part in determining the behaviour – or otherwise – of your undoubtedly charming child. However hard you may try to raise your offspring in a gender-free fashion, there will come a time when your dearly beloved dot will unashamedly show her (I can only imagine) pink or his (boy, have I been there!) true blue colours. Barbie or Ben 10, gender will out.

★ ★ ★

116

Prior to – and even immediately after – the arrival of our first boy, the FOB and I had both feet planted firmly in the 'nurture, not nature' camp. We got out my dolls, took out his garage and painted the 'baby room' a non-committal yellow. Whether boy or girl, it wouldn't matter. We would treat our firstborn in exactly the same way, whether with willy or without, would expose him/her to the same experiences and excitement and he/she would grow up to be beautifully balanced.

Our number-one mini-male has other ideas.

For the first twelve months or so, Sensible Son is no different from any of his female friends. He laughs, he cries, he crab crawls. Apart, of course, from the ever-present risk of 'willy wash' and thereafter cut-up cloths, there is no discernible difference between my life as a MOB and the neonatal experiences of my many MOG mates.

All that, however, is about to change.

It's a beautiful autumn day, crisp and crunchy, and my boddler boy and I set off for our daily dawdle round the woods. He clasps his hand in mine, and we meander up the path, stopping for me to catch my once-again pregnant breath, for him to pick up woodlice and worms. I watch as he examines with fascination the tiny creatures he so patiently pursues and wish that this innocent interest could be bottled for future, less stimulating, mature moments. Eventually, he's had enough of the mini-beasts, and picks up . . . a stick.

Tottering over to the side of the path, Sensible Son centres himself squarely, raises his podgy arm and pauses. And then, without warning, he starts beating seven bells out of an innocent bush, grunting gleefully as he pounds it to a pulp.

'Hey, stop that!' I say, lumbering over and removing the now broken branch from his grip. 'We don't hit plants, do we?' He looks up at me blankly and grins, before stooping to pick up another weapon of wood.

My unsullied offspring is fourteen months old. He's never been to playgroup. Never watched anything other than sensitive CBeebies. Never witnessed – to my certain knowledge – anyone else beating up a bush or even brandishing a branch.

I am horrified.

How has this happened to my pacifist poppet? A house full of teddies and trains – not a single gun, stick or sword in sight. And yet here he is, my blue-eyed bundle of snuggles, demonstrating a preternatural tendency towards gratuitous violence and acting, to all intents and purposes, like a thug. No longer behaving like any old boddler, but a *boy*.

I share my concern that I have quite possibly bred a bulldog at the next Mixed Mothers' cathartic coffee morning. An older and wiser Perfect Pair listens carefully to my tale of weapons and woe.

'Have you tried the hairbrush yet?' she asks with a knowing chuckle. I shake my head, indicating my son's still stubbornly bald one.

'No, not to brush his hair with . . . for the testosterone test!'

A test? For testosterone? Entirely unnecessary, I'd say, given recent experience. Still . . .

The 'TT' had apparently been the brainchild of Perfect Pair's own mother. A wholly unscientific, yet, to her mind, surprisingly substantive piece of gender research.

'When your daughter is two,' her Pop Professor mum had suggested, 'hand her a doll and a hairbrush. Retreat from the room and observe the results. When your son is the same age, repeat the experiment exactly as above. Watch and learn, sweetheart, watch and learn!'

Ever the dutiful daughter, she'd done as she was told.

Toddler girl had taken the brush and gently combed the doll's hair until her luscious locks gleamed like those of a proverbial princess. Every inch a mum in the making.

Toddler boy, meanwhile, had grasped the brush in one hand, the doll in the other and set about successfully (and scarily) decapitating the doll. Not exactly nurturing, but, in the proof of the pudding and in the Pop Prof's opinion, entirely predictable, and *natural*, boy behaviour.

I grasp at this double-edged-sword explanation with a mixture of relief and apprehension. Relief that my son is not, after all, an *Omen* anomaly; apprehension that if I'm to accept her assertion that boys *will* be boys, the stick incident could well be the beginning of the fairly ferocious end.

And as my gang of guys has grown from one to two to three, I have indeed come to support her suggestion that however much you encourage equality or adopt a unisex approach, however hard you try to foster the feminine or even push the pink, deep down inside their mini-male minds, a boy will be – forever – true boy.

So, in the absence of palaces, hair grips and handbags, our garden is now a battlefield of balls. Where once was a lawn is now Western Front, what once was a bench is now full-time bunker. Even the ancient apple tree is a makeshift lookout. With a moratorium on 'real' toy guns (will our weapons ban turn them into gun-touting loonies or push them instead to be peace-loving pacifists, or will it make not a blind bit of difference in the important long term?), our boys deploy conker cannons, hoard crabapple ammo, spend hour upon hour whittling weapons of wood.

With the exciting addition of other soldier sons, the newly formed boy brigade attacks anything that moves.

'Boys will be boys, hey?' sighs Extreme MOB, mother of the

rushed-in reinforcements, as we shelter, ever hopeful, under an un-protective parasol.

Her smallest son dishes out a particularly potent thump to Feisty Fellow; he roars his disapproval and prepares to strike back. Rising to stem the escalating counter-insurgency, I narrowly avoid having inches shaved off my backside by a dangerously sharp stick. Extreme MOB, blissfully blind to the almost certainly ensuing bloodbath, dodges a badly (or possibly not) aimed apple.

'Hmmm,' I acquiesce, eyeing the army which is preparing an assault on our out-of-bounds back door. 'Hey . . . don't even think about going inside!' I yell, leaving them absolutely and obviously no room for manoeuvre. Sensing defeat, they rapidly switch strategy and head for the hills.

For while outdoors, I admit, my life may well be toppled by testosterone, indoors, I refuse to relent. Indoors – as far as boy behaviour is concerned, at least – MOB rules.

Thus, statute Number One in my book of beliefs:

No sticks whatsoever may enter my abode. Or swords. Or frankly anything that bears even the faintest resemblance to the aforementioned objects. The insides of a kitchen towel roll, the tube left over after all the wrapping paper has been used up, even – on occasion – a rolled-up camping mat. All potential weapons of mass destruction (with the obvious exception of the camping mat, which now lives cheek by jowl with a hungry plague of mice in the shed) are swiftly disposed of in the recycling bins, before any damage can be done or chaos come about.

And thus, Number Two non-negotiable regulation:

No balls may live within this wise woman's walls. Rubber balls, exercise balls, bouncy balls, even balloons. The mere presence of round, rubber objects appears to incite uncontrollable lunacy of the highest degree. I once had a highly embarrassing experience at the house of a Perfect Pair involving a large blue birthing ball, a spiral staircase and a crystal chandelier. While the chandelier's owner was extremely understanding, I still feel faintly nauseous when at the scene of the crime. Balls and boys inevitably end in tears . . . and they (the tears) are most often mine. So, balls are confined to outside, and cannot be brought in.

It is possible that you might read these rules as proof of my aversion to any form of enjoyment or as overwhelming evidence of my predilection for power. I prefer to view my anti-anarchic approach as a way of ensuring that, amid my potentially manic male maelstrom, both my sanity and my walls remain partially intact.

On occasion, however, you, like me, may be seduced into a rare relaxation of these sanity-saving rules. You may choose, despite knowing better, to relinquish command and control. You may even find yourself discounting – temporarily – the sex of your son.

Fear not.

You can count on your boy offspring to alert you – possibly vocally and quite probably in public – to any momentary lapse of *Pink* Floyd reason.

It's Binary Boy's third birthday. The day dawns beautifully sunny and disappointingly early.

'Can I open my presents now?' he booms beside the bed. 'Pleeeze, pleeezze!'

'Of course you can, sweetheart,' I grunt, clambering out of bed and ensuring that sufficient cold air wafts under the covers to wake the still-snoring FOB.

'Come on, Evans,' I cajole, 'present-opening time!'

He pulls the duvet over his head and threatens to slumber on.

'Now!' I cry, removing the duvet completely and holding it just beyond his reach. He groans defeat and climbs into his clothes.

Five minutes later, Binary Boy is wallowing in wrapping paper, his gifts and their tags separated irrevocably, and now covering the carpet. 'One at a time' is apparently not a concept which appeals to the average three-year-old male.

'What's this?' he asks, holding up a large cardboard box. I look at the box, read the words on the side.

'Oh,' I say. 'It's nothing . . . it's a bit too old for you. We'll just put it away . . .'

'No, Mummeee, what is it? What is it?' he shrieks, sensing my reluctance and realising that this could, therefore, be something very interesting indeed.

I look at my husband, glumly. Equally glum, he shuffles to the shed to fetch a pump.

Ten minutes later, Binary Boy is bouncing round our too-small sitting room on the fully inflated 'Space Hopper'. His legs dangle helplessly around its Santa Claus belly and I'm hoicking him into the air, again . . . and again.

'This is fun!' he shrieks as we cavort round the room, crushing paper and presents. 'Higher! Faster!'

'Your turn,' I pant at the FOB. He opens his eyes from where he sits snoozing, stiffly stands up and begins to bounce.

'I want a go too!' announces a now not entirely Sensible Son, seeing that his younger brother's having far too much fun. 'My go, now. My go!' He races towards the orange ball, grabs a handle and begins to wrestle it from his unexpectedly strong sibling.

'Now then, boys . . . calm down. *Calm down*!' I minister. 'Let go will you, Sensible Son. It is your brother's birthday, after all. He'll let you have a go in a minute, won't you, Birthday Boy?'

Birthday Boy shakes his head. Eldest son prepares to attack again, taking a run-up this time and stamping painfully on Feisty Fellow's hand. Feisty Fellow begins to wail, although I can hardly hear it above the Koala Brother cries that are now emanating from the throats of sons numbers one and two.

'Right,' says the FOB authoritatively and eventually, taking charge of both the situation and the wayward orange beast. 'Enough!'

Taking the ball by the horns, he throws it out of the back door and into the garden, where, in my opinion, it rightly belongs.

His sons are stunned – temporarily – by their father's unusually tough tone. For a few seconds there's an uncertain silence, before the outraged wailing begins once again. Now I know, I think to myself, why inside MOB rules!

In the midst of this madness, the phone rings. My uncle, FOB of three (now towering) twenty-something sons, is calling to wish Binary Boy many happy returns. 'And are you doing anything special for your birthday?' I hear him ask the suddenly compliant Birthday Boy.

'We's goin' out for lunch!' he announces proudly.

I hear Uncle FOB splutter on the end of the line. 'You? Lunch? Out?'

'Yes,' I shout at the receiver, 'why, what's wrong with that?' I might be chained to the sink most of the time, but even this galley slave deserves the occasional day off.

'We didn't take our boys out to eat in public until they were . . . oooh, at least in double figures!' he reminisces. Then he smells my fear. 'Still, I'm sure yours will be fine; it's different these days, isn't it? Everything's much more family-friendly. Anyway, must go. Best of luck!' he says, getting off the phone a touch too quickly.

Luck? The FOB and I look at each other, perplexed. A family-friendly restaurant, two adults, three children. What's not to like?

'Wow, look at that!' my husband and I say in stereo a few hours later, as the boys' iced water arrives with plastic giraffes protruding from plastic tops. The waitress comes back bearing pencils and paper.

'Oooh!' gurgle the boys gleefully, grabbing crayons and cups. The FOB and I take the menus and sit back. With premature pride, we smile at each other, enjoying the enthusiastic response to their luxury lunch.

Two minutes later.

'Never mind,' I soothe as Sensible Son prepares to erupt. Icy liquid cascades like Niagara from his now crushed cup on to the table and thereafter into his lap. I pinch a handful of extra napkins from the thankfully empty next-door table. 'Though I did say you wouldn't be able to drink it with the giraffe still *in* there, didn't I?' He nods solemnly, dabs his sodden shorts and begins to sniff. 'It's only water,' I say rapidly, fearing meltdown. 'It'll dry.'

Binary Boy watches his brother from the other side of the table and hastily removes his four-legged friend.

'That's right!' we encourage, as he successfully slurps without spilling a drop. He stops and screws up his nose.

'I don't like ice!' he announces loudly. He removes the top and attempts to fish the offending objects from his cup. 'No ice!' he protests, trying to grasp a slippery cube which skedaddles to the floor. 'That's better!' he says, replacing the top and finishing his drink. 'Need a wee now!' The FOB is despatched to look for the loos.

Feisty Fellow promptly disappears under the table.

'What are you up to under there?' I ask, grabbing the back of his dungarees and trying to hoist my heffalump back on to the bench. 'What have you got in your mouth, young man?' I say, risking life and limb to force his tiny teeth apart.

An ice cube, covered almost entirely with hair, dust and dirt, plops out of his mouth and on to the table. Feisty Fellow chomps on. 'What else have you got in there?' Obediently, he spits out a partially digested wax crayon and a glob of paper. 'Is that it?' I ask, hopefully. He grins.

Red-faced now with embarrassment and exertion, I scramble back up on to the bench, strap Feisty Fellow safely into the high chair and struggle to regain both my breath and composure. I look around the restaurant.

The next-door table has been filled – calmly and quietly – by a multiple MOG and her gaggle of girls. So this is what an *oestrogen* outing looks like, I think, watching their activities with the fascination of a foreigner.

The girls fold their coats, twiddle their hair and fall upon their crayons, like my boys do upon biscuits. Then, behind cupped hands, they giggle and whisper as they examine the menu, discussing – at length – what it is that they want.

My observations are interrupted by Sensible Son. 'Where's my food?' he moans, never at his best when he's waiting to be fed. 'I'm the hungriest boy in the whole wide world!'

I glare at him, but *now* is not the time to tackle *that* topic. I add it to my mental 'discuss later' list and take an increasingly desperate deep breath.

Shortly afterwards, and not a moment too soon, our order arrives.

The boys demolish their burgers in a matter of minutes. The plates of fries go with similar speed.

'Slow down, guys . . .' I advocate with mock severity. 'It's not a race, you know!'

They grunt, barely raising their forks, let alone their eyes, from their almost gleaming plates. 'Can I have some a' your pizza, Mummy?' chomps the Birthday Boy, helping himself to a slice of my Margherita. I nod automatically at our apparently hollow-legged son, my own secret weapon in the fight against flab.

Meanwhile, on Oestrogen Isle at the next-door table, the MOG addresses one of her daughters in a low, wheedling whisper.

'Just one more mouthful, sweetheart . . . for me? Preety preety pleeeze?' She dangles a single penne in front of her daughter's resolutely closed mouth. Her daughter looks at her, entirely uninterested, shakes her head and continues to colour. The well-rounded MOG sighs loudly – 'I don't know why I bother to bring you out!' – forks up the pasta and finishes it herself.

Back on Planet MOB, we munch our way swiftly through pudding. I ask for the bill before the boys have time to beg for seconds of ice cream and sprinkles.

A few moments later, the waitress returns. 'The bill, madam . . . and for your boys . . .' I eye the bunch of balloons she's holding happily above her head, and look worriedly out of the window. I have another of my parental premonitions, aware of the almost certain calamity that will occur the moment we step outside into the too-windy world.

'Ermm . . .' I begin. Too late.

'Boon! Boon!' shrieks Feisty Fellow, clapping his sauce-sticky hands.

'Yeah, balloons . . . we love balloons!' yell the bigger boys, equally excited.

Don't we just! I nod, reluctantly. 'Shall Daddy hold them for you till we get to the car?'

Three boys glower at me, daring me to take away their blessed balloons.

'OK,' I give in, palms to the sky. 'Oh-kay.'

Three minutes later, the balloons are wending their way towards the Isle of Wight. Feisty Fellow howls as he watches them disappear into the distance. Binary Boy clutches his stomach and says he feels sick. Sensible Son wails along behind, his giraffe-soaked shorts still haven't dried and now, so the world hears, his 'willy is wet'.

'Well, wasn't that fun?' jollies my glass-half-full FOB. I gaze at him incredulously, trying to work out exactly how many years we have to go until *our* boys reach double figures, and are finally fit for public consumption.

Oldest Friend turned MOG, then MOB, thus Perfect Pair, comes back to visit.

Her son brings his wellies and disappears immediately into the depths of the garden.

Her Gorgeous Girl comes clutching her 'very own baby', complete with 'very own grobag'. She struggles to get her inflex-ible friend into the mini sleepsuit.

'Go on,' I suggest to Sensible Son, 'give her a hand!'

He eyes the doll sceptically, but then, ever eager to please, sets about accomplishing this unfamiliar task. Thirty seconds later, the doll has been stuffed into its suit, arms pinioned firmly and uncomfortably to its sides.

'Poor dolly . . . take her arms out!' admonishes Gorgeous Girl.

Obediently, he pulls at the 'baby's' limbs – and drops it, head first, on the floor. One arm falls off.

'Oh dear,' he states, eyeing the dismembered doll. 'Your baby's dead!'

Gorgeous Girl stares at her infant with deeply distressed eyes. She starts to sob.

'Aw, don't worry,' soothes Sensible Son gently. 'It'll be fine . . . it's OK.'

Oh, I think, MOB proud: how lovely, how kind, how utterly empathetic.

My biggest boy regards the now defunct doll. Suddenly, his face lights up. 'Shall we have a funeral?'

You can lead a boy to Barbie, sure, but you *cannot* make him pink.

Ten entirely empirical and irritatingly stereotypical reasons why it's marvellous being a MOB

- The needs of a lad are simple and straightforward: exercise, discipline, lunacy and love. Oh, and a never-ending supply of Scooby snacks.
- You'll always be in profit at a 'Pick your own'. Although, of course, they may not let you come back.
- Boys are fascinated, not horrified, by your cellulite and wrinkles.
- You can tickle a boy until he pees his pants. And he'll still come back for more.
- One day he'll bend down and kiss the top of your head. He may even wipe his nose before he does so.
- No hair bands. No grips. No plaits. Nits. Need I say more?
- Your boy can go almost anywhere with an out-of-bed head. And still look lovely.
- What you spend at the supermarket, you'll get back on clothes.
- You'll never have to read *Milly-Molly-Mandy* again and realise how rubbish it actually was. Probably.
- OK, OK, so you'll never have the stripy tights. But then again, you'll never have to get them on to her when she's still wet from swimming, will you? I rest my case.

Putting on a party that's fit for your Prince

From laser quests, to quad bikes, to hiring a pool, opportunities abound when it comes to parties for your Prince. But if you, like me, are just a little bit stingy and a big bit mad, you could choose instead to organise your own. So here are my essential ingredients for a homemade Birthday Boy bash.

1. Space
Enough for the party-goers to let off steam, but not enough to let them get lost.

2. Structure
Be it an obstacle course, a magic show or a good old egg and spoon, create a focus for what can otherwise degenerate into a lunacy of lads. Or maybe this is just me and my penchant for power . . . So, if you like lunacy, be my focus-free guest.

3. Control
Confiscate presents on arrival to avoid any 'Does-this-present-go-with-this-card . . . or-that-one?' confusion. Under five, your son just can't stop himself tearing open his gifts. And over five, he'll realise that anonymous presents mean fewer 'Thank-you' letters to write.

4. Competition
Organise a football match, do a treasure hunt or play a plain pass the parcel. The winners will forever hail your boy's bash as 'the Best'. Be prepared though, for dealing with the disappointment of any little losing lads. A consolation Cadbury's usually does the trick.

5. Food
Get yourself a cash-and-carry card in anticipation of the event. Take a trolley and fill it to the brim with additive-infused crisps,

sugar-laden sweets and large quantities of cola. Add the odd chocolate spread sarnie or two for good measure. Then sit back with a cuppa, while your gang of party guys talk calmly at the table. Err, not. Alternatively, stick to boring breadsticks and water. Your choice.

6. Restraint
Do not put the cookies and cakes out at exactly the same time as the cucumber and carrots. Shockingly, boys do not share your five-a-day fixation.

7. Planning
Avoid bouncy balls/whistles/bubbles in your lads' party bags. While the boys undoubtedly will love them, their mothers – and the smaller sibling who is hit with/tormented by/drinks the aforementioned – will not. If you must do party bags, do the environment a favour and buy them a book.

8. Emotion
The birthday boy will cry – at least once – at his own party. There's something very wrong if he doesn't. And Cyndi Lauper did. So it must be OK.

9. Realism
A pottery-painting party may sound like a lovely idea. But, really . . . bull . . . china shop . . . point taken?

10. Enjoy
Your boy party may, or may not, go off with a bang. Depending on your theme, this may, or may not, be a good thing. Either way, remember that you're now off the hook for another twelve months. Or eleven months, thirty days and five minutes, to be precise.

LESSON 8:

Bruises are good, but blood is bad

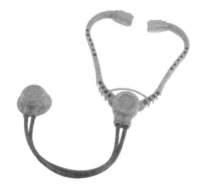

Sticks and stones may break their bones, chants the age-old adage. So, and in accordance with MOB rule, I banish them from my house. But it doesn't mention bikes, or indeed maps, anywhere. And by the time I realise the almost certain perils of a MOB on the move, it's already far too late to learn.

Let me set the scene.

An idyllic summer's day, a happy family bike ride along a country lane. Sensible Son and Binary Boy bomb along on their mud-splattered Raleighs with the FOB in front; Feisty Fellow is strapped in his seat on the back of my own seen-better-days mountain bike. We round yet another corner and I stop to look at the map.

'Are you sure it's this way?' I ask the FOB, determined to challenge the notion that while men (blatantly) don't listen, women (still up for debate) can't read maps.

'What's that?' he asks, simultaneously skidding to a halt beside me and confirming the veracity of at least one half of the sexual stereotype.

'I said,' I repeat, turning the map around to reflect the direction of travel and inadvertently substantiating the second part of the statement, 'are you sure this is the right way?'

'Quite sure!' reassures the FOB, preparing to take off in pursuit of his elder sons.

Turning to catch sight of his father, Feisty Fellow shifts his bottom just enough to tip the balance of my stationary bike. Desperately, I grapple with the handlebars to try to stop the inevitable fall, but try as I might, my lack of muscles just can't cope with the momentum and mass. The bike topples to the ground. My smallest son instinctively shoots out his arm to break the fall; there's an ominous silence followed by a blood-curdling scream.

Grappling with his straps, the FOB and I quickly release our battered boy from his seat. I cradle him on the grass.

'Oooh, my poor wee man,' I lull. 'I'm so sorry . . . I just couldn't hold you.' Gradually, his screams downgrade to mere wails as he stares pitifully at his earth-shattering arm. 'Shall Mummy kiss it better?' I attempt to soothe. To no avail. He continues to wail.

I look at my husband. 'What on earth are we going to do now?' I ask. We are miles from the car, hours from a hospital, we've no phone and no plan.

'Look, it's probably as much the shock of falling over as his actual arm that's upsetting him,' he suggests sensibly. 'Let's bike back to the village and have a rest and an ice cream . . . that normally does the trick!'

'You're probably right. OK – let's go,' I agree, not wanting to spoil a – till now – perfect day, but at the same time dubiously eyeing our still-sobbing soldier.

'Yay, ice creams, ice creams!' chant his food-focused elder brothers, quickly remounting their bikes. The now far-from-Feisty Fellow continues to alternate between hiccups and howls. This does not bode well.

Half an hour later, smallest son fails the thus far extremely successful triple choc chip 99 rescue remedy. Despite our encouragement, he's unable to hold the cornet with his limp left arm. Rivulets of molten chocolate and sobbing snot run down his chin as he wobbles his cone dangerously in his other hand. He looks at me mournfully with red-rimmed eyes. My maternal stomach lurches painfully and the FOB and I, finally, reluctantly, give each other the defeated nod.

Not for the first (and definitely not the last) time, we make our way towards the joy that is A&E on a post-rugby Sunday night.

A week later and Feisty Fellow is disconcertingly swift to learn the many 'sympathy-vote' benefits of the broken bone. No, he can't possibly dress himself any more. No, he really can't manage to hold an apple, but a biscuit, well, OK. No, he doesn't think he can walk to school – the pushchair would suit him much better, thanks. And anyway, hadn't that 'nice nurse at the hospital' told him to 'rest'?

'Are you sure,' I mutter in his ear as I puff to school, 'you haven't lost the use of your legs . . . as well as your arm?'

In the playground, a flutter of mummy moths descend on him and his incapacitated arm, as I kiss and drop the bigger boys.

'Oooh, what happened to yooooou?' they ask sympathetically, eyeing the immaculate cobalt cast that proudly protrudes from his rolled-up sleeve.

'Mummy did it!' he announces to the cooing audience, drawn ever closer by his doleful doe eyes and slightly pathetic, lopsided appearance.

I smile what I can only hope is an appropriately blameless 'out-of-the-mouths-of-babes' excuse, before propelling both the patient, and his pushchair, swiftly home.

The trick, I learn later from more accident-experienced MOBs, is to know the quickest route to A&E, but to avoid being on first-name terms with the staff. Extreme MOB fills me in on outpatients' etiquette.

'If your name comes up automatically on the computer, it

doesn't look good. If they don't have to ask for it, it really isn't great. And if you have your own allocated bed, prepare for a call from social services!' She speaks with the slightly worrying wisdom of one who knows.

'Oh yes,' she reminisces matter-of-factly, 'I've spent more time in outpatients than you've had tepid tea! Contusions, concussions, split knees and split lips, peas up noses and in ears . . . I could easily go on. If I just had one boy, it'd probably look bad enough, but once you've got multiple males, you spend so much time in triage, even *you* begin to question your own innocence.' I gawp and gulp, realising that I appear to have got away rather lightly with only *one* broken bone to date. 'Still,' she adds, casually scraping a slathering of Play-Doh from her smallest tot's tongue, 'I suppose it's only to be expected when you're surrounded by sons!'

And so I reflect on my first 'boy break' and on Extreme MOB's more extensive medical experiences. I'm somehow shocked by both her – and indeed my own – certainly resigned, verging on relaxed, reactions to our A&E exposure.

Would our responses to our wounded warriors have been different had we been blessed with sugar-and-spice girls instead of ants-in-pants boys? Were we surrounded with careful creatures who play calmly, sit still, stay put and not lunatic lads who can fall over nothing, climb curtains and walls? Has the plethora of inexplicable bruises, agonisingly skinned knees and gory gashes made us immune (and maybe a little blasé?) to the potential dangers and damage of a boy-ballistic household? I'm sure that I read in one of my manuals that optimistic women tend to give birth to boys, but is this because MOBs need a kind of blind faith, a positive frame of mind to cope with the frightening realities of 'boys will be boys'?

I smile, remembering one such recent MOB moment. Perched on a bench next to a mother and her two small sons at the local swimming pool, I had watched as her dynamo duo threatened to strangle each other in an overblown bear hug.

'Hey, be gentle,' suggested the MOB calmly from the sidelines.

'But we love each ovva!' protested her alpha male. His younger brother, slowly turning blue, didn't reply.

'Well, love each other a *little* less vigorously, will you . . . and wait till we're home,' she said, coolly untangling two arms from a neck. Alpha male loosened his grip – just a fraction – and the colour returned to beta boy's face.

His MOB mother turned to me, motioning towards her eldest son. 'He's just turned four,' she said, before adding, somewhat unnecessarily, 'too many visits from the Testosterone Fairy . . . or that's what the Steve Biddulph boy bible says!' She smiled serenely and swan-glided on. I nodded knowingly in her unruffled wake.

For according to both my well-read books and my own, at times all-too-horrible history, small boys appear to be pathologically programmed to be physical, to do damage not only to themselves but to the ones they love most, on an all-too-rugged and -regular basis.

From the moment the scientifically substantiated hit of hormones quite literally kicks in at around four years old, loopy lads struggle to control their XY tempers, while adults desperately seek channels for their apparently limitless energy. Thus, playgrounds, pre-schools and parks ring to cries of 'Slow down/ Get up/Don't jiggle/Sit still', while the boys, tanked up on testosterone and action-oblivious, 'play' on.

The seasoned MOB, meanwhile, rises above the riot, blissfully aware that in her sons' wild, wacky world, bundling and bear hugs are proof of their passion, beating each other up is reserved for best friends, a 'love punch' in the gonads confirms that they care.

Not for nothing, I reflect, was it Humpty Dumpty who fell inexplicably off that wall, Georgie Porgie who made his female friends cry with overblown affection, Jack who ended up in casualty with concussion. Jill, presumably, tripped daintily after, trying to administer first aid to her boisterous brother.

And so, I accede, it probably *is* true that I have come to view the bumps and bruises that are part and parcel of living with my boys as – while far from enviable – pretty much inevitable. That I am developing almost total immunity to the extra-large quantities of guy guts and gore.

'No "*bumped my head*" sticker today, folks?' I say, surprised, as my sons hurtle towards me at the end of the school day. One by one they shake their heads. Then Sensible Son/Binary Boy/ Feisty Fellow (delete as applicable) says, 'Oh, I forgot,' and reaches into his bag.

'This is for you!' he says happily, thrusting an '*ice-was-administered-no-lasting-damage*' disclaimer into my hands before careering over to his mates, narrowly avoiding both an unsuspecting grandparent and the prominent root of a gnarly tree.

On Planet MOB, my boys and their buddies wear their '*Keep-an-eye-on-me*' stickers with a kind of 'rite-of-passage' pride.

And while stickers mean status, bruises – the bigger, the blacker, the better – bring kid-cred and kudos.

'Where did *those* come from *this* time?' I ask my eldest, any day of the week, as he strips for the shower.

'What?' he asks, craning his neck to see what particular part of his anatomy is offending his mother today. Enormous blotches cover his legs; his skin looks like the dappled pelt of a piebald pony. 'Oh . . . those,' he says, part proud, part perplexed.

'Dunno . . . could've been from yesterday when I walked into the table; or maybe it was Friday when I tripped over the step. Hang on, no – it was football last Monday . . . I was tackling Tom. Anyway – doesn't hurt!'

I shake my head – what else can I do? – and mutter, 'Ouch!' Despite the many years of being desensitised to disaster, I still can't help cringing inwardly in unwanted empathy.

But while bruises may be pretty much par for my boys' nonchalant course, the presence of blood, apparently, requires not just authentic empathy, but concerned sympathy – in king-size buckets. At the first drop of the red stuff, my mini-man-flu-men-in-the-making take to the skinned-knee stage with all the overblown pathos of a Shakespearian tragedy.

'I'm dying!' they gasp theatrically at the sight of a scratch.

'Don't come near me, don't touch me,' they scream as I search under asphalt for the source of what ails.

'There's BLOOD!' they howl as I dab at their elbow/forehead/knee with a tissue that might just pass muster as clean to reveal a microscopic, and far from fatal, hole in their suddenly hypersensitive skin. 'Woe's me, oh woe's me!' they sigh, before taking to their beds. My Othellos open their mouths hopefully, for compassion and grapes. To their outraged surprise, little is forthcoming.

So, while they, and indeed I, may be blasé about bruises, the potential for boy blood meltdowns should not be underestimated. Thus, in addition to the original 99 rescue remedy, I now have extra resources up my medicinal MOB sleeve. My handbag bulges with save-the-day Savlon, placating plasters, Piriton and Calpol. My head bulges with distraction tactics ('I know your finger's about to fall off, but cor . . . did you just see that really cool car?') for bloodied boys. And I never leave home without an emergency bag of feel-better Buttons. However hardened to horror, it pays to be prepared for the son who is only, after all, a hypochondriac *bloke*-to-be . . . with BLOOD.

Meanwhile, amid the daily damage of the bruises and bashes, Feisty Fellow and his cast struggle valiantly on.

As the outer shell turns a deep-sea blue and his shrivelled-up skin starts to ever so slightly smell, I begin to count the days to when he can, once again, tuck in his duvet and put on his *own* pants. Like the well-trodden path to his helpless assistance, my bedside manner is beginning to wear pretty thin.

Amazingly, and bearing an uncanny resemblance to a purportedly man-flu male at the prospect of the pub, he makes a miraculous recovery when we arrive for the holidays, at Good-life Gran's.

Our boys are extremely fortunate to have two types of 'outdoor-active' Grandparents of Boys.

The paternal (oh-so-attractively abbreviated) GOBs, on the one hand, partake in prison visiting, boating and long walks. The resultant mixture of crime, slime and grime make them natural hits with their gory grandsons.

The maternal GOBs, on the other, focus on finding fossils and rearing animals; the ensuing combination of danger and dung hold obvious attractions for our competitive hounds.

And thus it is that on half-term holidays, we pack our bags and boots, and head off to one of the two respective (and receptive) sets of grandparents. Today is the turn of the Fossil-Farmer GOBs.

After three hours of 'I spy', I pull on the handbrake and breathe in a lungful of deepest Devon air. The elder boys scramble from the car and I turn to help my still-invalid son.

No need.

With hitherto unimaginable dexterity, Feisty Fellow unclips himself from his car seat, wrenches open the heavy door and runs straight into the arms of his Good-life Gran.

'How's your arm?' she enquires tenderly.

'It'sh still quite shore,' he lisps, shooting accusatory glances at his guilt-ridden mother. 'It will get better shoon I fink.'

Predictably, perhaps, it rapidly does.

The following morning as I stumble bleary-eyed into the kitchen to switch on the kettle, the 'wounded warrior' stands poised for action in his freshly washed boiler suit, a plastic bag tied around his cast with a fraying length of orange binder twine.

'I thought we'd better *try* to keep it as clean as we can while we go out and feed the animals,' explains Good-life Gran. I nod, heartened by her unusually attentive approach. Cleanliness has never been a priority in this self-sufficient household, where it's worth sniffing the milk to check whether it is destined for humans, lambs or the plug hole and where the encrustations on the breakfast bowl may well be chick pellets and not Grape Nuts as you'd first naively believed.

Still, with just over a week to go until 'cast off', it pays to be prudent.

Hand in be-casted hand, Good-life Gran and Feisty Fellow head out into the cool morning air. Clasping a mug of steaming coffee to the front of her pyjamas, this gratefully redundant Florence Nightingale heads back to bed.

Two mornings later, however, my mother has a confession to make.

'I'm really sorry,' she begins. I hold my breath – this sounds bad. Although at this time of day, I think, automatically glancing at my watch and searching for my shoes, the waiting time at the local outpatients department shouldn't be *too* bad.

'Who is it?' I ask, fearing the worst, and wondering whether yet another A&E trip will warrant my inclusion on the 'at-risk' register of negligent MOBs.

She looks at me, confused. 'No, the boys are fine – really. Honestly, I don't know why you worry so much!'

I snort my retort like one of her pigs.

She continues, 'It's just that we were in such a hurry this morning that, I, um . . . well, I forgot to put the bag on over Feisty Fellow's cast. And well . . . we . . . err . . . had a *bit* of an accident.'

Right on cue, my youngest son enters the kitchen, breathless, beaming and brandishing a cast which now looks – and smells – like putrid papier mâché.

'I falled in the pig pen!' he exclaims, seemingly ecstatic at his good fortune. 'Look, my arm's changed colour!'

I stare at his humming stump, wondering how on earth I will explain the top coat of manure on my supposedly 'taking-it-easy' child's cast to an urban orthopaedist.

As a MOB, *I* may be able to turn a blind eye to the rowdy realities of living with lads, but unless our doctor happens to be improbably devoid of both sight and smell, I fear I may be about to take centre stage in my own highly embarrassing tragedy. Social services – here we come.

A few days later, I am sitting in the hospital waiting room, eyeing the screen which is about to inform me that my time is up. Feisty Fellow squirms on my lap.

'Will it hurt when they saw my arm off?' he asks. Distracted, I reassure him that the procedure will take just seconds and will be completely pain-free, unlike my own ongoing state of anxiety.

What if my efforts to scrub the cast clean have been less than successful? What if the staff sniff suspiciously as the pong of a porker assaults their antibacterial noses? What if the removal of the cast reveals – oh woe is me indeed – not just a shrunken sun-starved arm, but the presence of poo?

As it turns out, our saw-wielding saviour has sons of her own. She is untroubled and unfazed by the outward appearance of the cast.

'I know what it's like,' she says as she dons her goggles and sets to work on Feisty Fellow's arm. 'It's nigh-on impossible to keep the kids quiet, let alone keep the cast clean . . . especially with boys!' I nod nervously, grateful for the understanding of a sister MOB, but all too aware that we're not quite out of the worry woods yet. 'All done!' she announces, brandishing the now redundant halves of plaster cast for all to see. I examine them quickly for incriminating evidence of harebrained neglect. Seeing none, I thank her, prolongedly and profusely, for her help.

'No problem,' she says, faintly bewildered by my out-of-proportion gratitude. 'Let's hope we don't see you back here again too soon!' she adds, smiling at my son, who is vigorously rubbing his newly released arm. Bowing low and bobbing backwards, I grab his other arm, and, like a criminal granted bail, get ready to flee.

I have my hand on the door when the doctor suddenly bends over and picks something up from under the stool where Feisty Fellow had sat so unusually still only minutes before. I watch, frozen, as she gazes intently at the object in her hand. She looks up at me; I look back at her. Even at this distance, and even in its decaying state, the curled up creature is all too recognisable as a maggot.

I give a Scooby Doo gulp. 'Boys will be boys, hey?' I suggest hopefully.

She raises her eyebrows, obviously unconvinced. Blood: fine; bruises: absolutely; even the odd broken bone is acceptable on an appropriately intermittent basis. But the unexpected arrival of our fur-less friend is pushing the understanding of even this MOB-familiar medic.

She looks at my son, she looks at the phone. I can tell she's torn between social services and sympathy. Slowly and surely, she makes her decision. Eyes fixed firmly on mine, she drops both cast and maggot meaningfully in the bin. They thud, case closed, to the floor.

Blasé I may be, optimistic I am, but even I know that if you don't want the heat, you should get out of the hospital. Without further ado, I seize my son and exit – swiftly – stage left.

Accident and emergency information every MOB should know

- Bumps and bruises are part of son street-cred.
- At around four years of age, the Testosterone Fairy comes and sprinkles hormones on to your previously biddable boy. So, when your tot turns overnight into a ferocious fiend who can trip over air, you can laugh – ever so lightly – in his outraged face, in the knowledge that his behaviour is entirely boy normal.
- You should never leave the house without feel-better Buttons.
- 'Miss' knows best. And if 'Miss' says that that teeny, tiny scratch needs a leg-length bandage and continual TLC, then she's right. And you're not.
- Savlon is magic: it can make absolutely anything better. But if you don't have Savlon, any cream will do.

When a Boy hurts himself

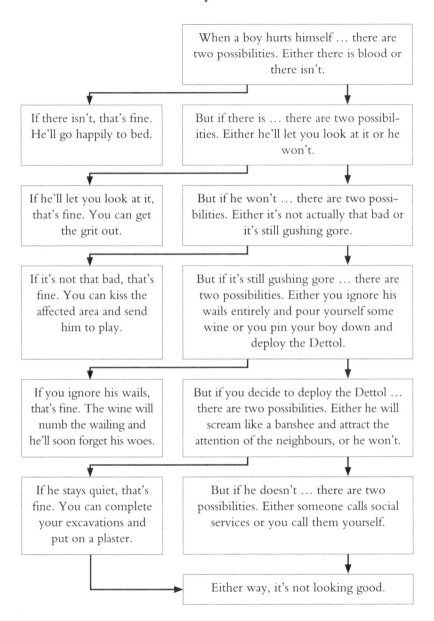

When a boy hurts himself ... there are two possibilities. Either there is blood or there isn't.

If there isn't, that's fine. He'll go happily to bed.

But if there is ... there are two possibilities. Either he'll let you look at it or he won't.

If he'll let you look at it, that's fine. You can get the grit out.

But if he won't ... there are two possibilities. Either it's not actually that bad or it's still gushing gore.

If it's not that bad, that's fine. You can kiss the affected area and send him to play.

But if it's still gushing gore ... there are two possibilities. Either you ignore his wails entirely and pour yourself some wine or you pin your boy down and deploy the Dettol.

If you ignore his wails, that's fine. The wine will numb the wailing and he'll soon forget his woes.

But if you decide to deploy the Dettol ... there are two possibilities. Either he will scream like a banshee and attract the attention of the neighbours, or he won't.

If he stays quiet, that's fine. You can complete your excavations and put on a plaster.

But if he doesn't ... there are two possibilities. Either someone calls social services or you call them yourself.

Either way, it's not looking good.

(With humble apologies to Sean Taylor & Nick Sharratt's highly addictive *When a Monster Is Born*)

There's no point saying life's not a competition. It is

It's Thursday, another Feisty Fellow and Best Boy Friend day, and I'm standing at the stove, making soup.

Feisty Fellow and his Best Boy Friend are lining up cars in the sitting room with slightly worrying psychotic precision. According to both manuals and other MOBs, however, this is entirely normal boy behaviour. And anyway, it can – and frequently does – occupy hours.

The calm is broken as an argument begins to escalate.

'My dad's bigger than yours!' grumps Feisty Fellow, crashing into one of Best Boy Friend's cars.

'Isnot! My dad's bigger than yours!' cries Best Boy Friend, launching a lorry at Feisty Fellow's truck.

'Is too, is too,' taunts my youngest. 'My dad's the biggest in the whole wide world!' He chucks a crane at the garage which lands, instead, alarmingly close to Best Boy Friend's head.

Best Boy Friend sensibly admits defeat. At six foot seven, the FOB has an unnaturally unfair advantage in the battle of the giants. But Best Boy Friend hasn't finished yet. 'Well . . .' he retaliates, 'my dad's defn'tly older than yours, anyway . . . so there. He's got *much* lesser hair than *your* dad!'

I suppress a smile at this (factually incorrect) observation and enter the fray.

'Hey boys . . . come on,' I say, plonking myself down on to the car-strewn carpet, a scrap heap of son squabbles. 'Calm down a bit, guys . . . it doesn't matter whose dad is biggest, whose dad is oldest, now does it?' They stare at me, huge eyes threatening to pool over with the emotion of their fight.

With reception teacher resolve, I try to explain.

'Some people are tall, like Feisty Fellow's dad, and some are short, like . . .'

'You!' concludes my son, helpfully.

'Yes, like . . . hang on, I'm absolutely average, I'll have you know! Well, almost average. Anyway . . . the point is, it's not all about being the tallest or the eldest . . . we're all different and that's absolutely fine. Life's not a competition, you know!'

Partially mollified, and presumably uninspired by my underwhelming insight into human psychology, the boys turn back to their garage.

'Well, your dad might be older, but my mum's fatter!' I hear Feisty Fellow hiss at his best mate's back.

I stop on my way to the kitchen, begin to turn – and then turn back, returning to the soup instead of my son.

Because I realise that I'm wrong there actually, very wrong. For while to my female mind it may not be all about competition, to my testosterone-infused tots it most certainly is. Being the oldest, the boldest, the fastest, the first, *really* matters to my mini-men and their mini-men mates. For boys, it seems, being the best matters . . . a lot.

I'm reminded of the incident and its implications some time later as Sensible Son plots his up-and-coming eighth birthday party at the dinner table. The preparations, and indeed the party, prove my point.

With 'only' two months to go until the 'Big Day', we talk of little else.

'Muum, please can I have a sleepover . . . pleezeee?'

'A sleepover? Really?' Visions of hordes of belligerent boys refusing to sleep swim unappetisingly in front of my eyes. 'What's wrong with a couple of hours during the day, pass the parcel, a cupcake and then home like everyone else?' He looks at me disparagingly. Quite a bit, apparently.

'Pleeze, Mum. I really want a sleepover, no one else has had one for their birthday . . . I'd be the first . . . it'd be *so* cool!'

Smelly undoubtedly, noisy absolutely, but 'cool'? I silently beg to differ.

'Well, who would you want to invite if we *did* say yes?' He senses I'm weakening and grins excitedly.

'Well, there's Tom, and there's Dick, oh and then, of course, Harry. And if they're coming, then Joe should, and his best friend Bloggs, too.' He reels off the names of each and every male member of his class – and arrives at eleven.

'Eleven? You want to have *eleven* boys in *our* house, *overnight?*'

'Well, no . . . it'd be fourteen, if you include me, Binary Boy and Feisty Fellow. And actually, not in the house . . . I was thinking more of the tent . . .'

This last he proposes as if chaos under canvas would in any way be preferable to bedlam in his bedroom.

I huff, I puff, we hum, we haw. And eventually, we give in.

Two weeks before the party.

'I've been thinking, Mum . . .' begins my firstborn smoothly, draping a long arm around my suddenly suspicious shoulders.

'Hmmm?'

'About my birthday . . . my party. Maybe you could write a mystery . . . you know . . . set around the village. Like *Secret Seven* . . . with clues to find, a crime to solve. It'd be so . . .'

'Cool?' I suggest.

'Awesome!' he finishes. 'It'd be awesome. No one else has

ever had their own story written specially for them. Will you, Mum? Will you?'

'A mystery, à la Blyton . . . just like that?' He nods his innocently alluring head.

I huff, I puff, I hum, I haw. Eventually, of course, I give in.

One week before the party.

We are eating Saturday bangers and mash.

'Muuum,' begins Sensible Son.

I raise my gaze, but continue to eat. I'm getting wise to this.

'Mum, can we have sausages at my party? But not like this . . . can we cook them ourselves? On a camp fire? On sticks? The boys would love it. It'd be so . . .'

Cool? Awesome? Unbelievably dangerous?

'Wicked. It'd be really wicked!' At least this exercise in party planning appears to be expanding his vocabulary more effectively than any literacy lesson.

I look at the FOB while I huff and I puff. He hums, he haws – but not for long. Sparkling at the prospect of pyromania and matches, my biggest boy FOB gives (delightedly) in.

Just like Binary Boy's third birthday, the day of the party dawns helpfully bright, but impossibly early. Call me paranoid, but there appears to be a pattern.

Unfortunately, given the night-time nature of the event, our overexcited offspring have a whole twelve hours to wait before the guests arrive. And for my 'me-first' men, my 'go-faster' guys, the likelihood of killing time without killing each other, their father or indeed their mother is not great.

By breakfast, we've blown up balloons and counted cups.

By lunchtime, we've spiked all the sausages and buttered the bread.

By teatime, we're shattered – and I, at least, am ready for bed. And then, one by one, the happy campers arrive.

As they're dropped off with sleeping bags, pillows and frankly decorative flannels, I am increasingly vindicated in my aforementioned belief that male children are actually dogs on two legs.

The FOB is deployed to calm the leaping lads.

'Right, who wants to help the Birthday Boy solve a mystery?' he bellows above the baying of the hounds.

'Me!' they scream, forming a circle around Sensible Son.

'Who wants to be on my team?' he shouts, beaming and relishing his five minutes of fame.

'Me! Me! I want to be on your team!' scream his friends, wagging their tails and scratching their balls.

I wade into the throng.

'Hang on, hang on . . . we don't need teams. This isn't a competition. It's a *mystery* . . . you'll need to work together to find the criminal, to solve the crime. It doesn't matter how fast you do it. It's not a race, you know!'

My eldest son's face falls for a moment. What does she mean there's no competition? Then he brightens.

'Well if it's not a race, then I'll be in charge. I'll be the leader!' he announces, pushing to the fore to line up his troops. Fearfully, I glance at Binary Boy.

'That's not fair!' he pipes up, predictably. 'You're always in charge! Why can't I go first for a change?'

I put my arm firmly round his cut-throat shoulders. 'You can go first when it's your birthday,' I say quietly, 'but *not* today!'

'Snot fair!' he pouts, before – thankfully – stepping sulkily into line. I sigh, relieved that at least this first sibling scene has been narrowly avoided. I check my watch. Only another fourteen hours to go.

And so the party, the night and the story unfold.

155

While the literary genius of my fake *Secret Seven* whizzes over their heads, and while I may not have intended it to be a 'me-first' mystery, my tale of stolen bicycles and devious culprits obviously appeals to the deepest instincts of this prehistoric pack.

Metaphorical spears at the ready, they race round the lanes from one clue to the next, decidedly fleeter of foot than their accompanying adults. Panting and puffing, the FOB and I clatter after them like the knackers-yard nags we are, desperately struggling to follow their scent.

Thankfully for us, even the fittest of adventurers cannot ignore a call of nature and thus we round the corner to find them stopped – en masse – to pee along a fence.

'Hold on . . . a minute . . .' I heave at the row of beautifully bared bottoms. 'Have you . . . actually . . . worked out where you're going next?' I'm anxious to know whether they are following the thread of my spellbinding story or merely running a race against an invisible, innate enemy. 'Well?' I ask again, as they drip themselves dry, 'do you know *what* you're doing . . . or *why*?'

Hands on hips, they gaze at me uncomprehendingly. Marge vs Homer, Thelma vs Fred. MOB vs Man.

Sensible Son is the first to break the silence. 'Let's go!' he commands. 'We need to get there first . . . and fast!' Fast? First? But why? What is the reason? Where is the rush?

I watch incredulously as, spurred on by inner voices substantially louder than my own logical tones, he and his tribe hurtle for the hills and who knows – or cares – where. The FOB and I bring up the rear.

A mere eighteen minutes later, the boys are apparently 'done'. They've found their clues, they've raced their roads, the mystery – for what it's worth – is well and truly solved. Job done, game over.

'What's next?' they demand, still as fresh as dogged daisies.

My husband and I are utterly exhausted.

The FOB has spent most of the mystery with an aggrieved Feisty Fellow on his now soaking shoulders.

'They wouldn't wait for me!' he howls, scattering mud and muck down his father's back. 'I wanted to go first . . . it's not faaaaiiiir!'

I, meanwhile, have been otherwise occupied, trying to restrain Binary Boy from toppling his fraternal 'top dog'.

'Why's he always the leader?' gripes my Miliband in the making. He nips, frustrated, at his elder brother's heels. 'It's not faaaaiiiir!'

I resist the urge to turn into my mother and retort superciliously that 'life isn't fair'. I'm not convinced this would cut ice with my over-riled Rottweilers.

As far as the all-important Birthday Boy is concerned, however, the mystery mission was, it appears, 'like, totally massive'.

'We won!' he shrieks delightedly, while his friends leap up at him, licking his face.

'So who was the thief, then?' I ask, relieved that at least one third of my offspring appears to have enjoyed the event, and flattered by the rest of the rabble's enthusiasm for my meticulously planned script.

For the second time that evening, we stare at each other in mutual incomprehension. Them: Tarzans; me: Jane.

Better late than never, the FOB springs innocently into this test–oestrogen impasse.

'Who wants to help me make the fire?' he asks, before adding, 'tell you what, let's see who can find the most logs first!'

Unlike me, it seems, he speaks their language.

Whooping and wailing, a flock of males dives into the dusk.

'Bagsy me have the first sausage!' yells Tom, Dick or maybe it was Harry, as they disappear from sight.

Sensible Son whispers urgently in his father's ear. 'Dad, if he's having the *first*, can I have the *biggest?*' The FOB gives Birthday Boy a tacit nod. But not, evidently, tacit enough.

'That's not faaaaiiiiir!' duet his brothers.

I shudder and head inside, to the uncompetitive comfort of my cosy cave.

And thus, as I watch my boys striving to skim the slimmest of stones, climbing to the top of the tallest tree, struggling to conquer the most precarious of peaks, I reflect – not for the first time – on their peculiar desire, nay *need,* to succeed.

Once again, I consult my boy bibles. Competition is good, they advocate; the will to win can motivate, stimulate, encourage boys to achieve and even excel. But – and here's my current boy bone of contention – they also need to be taught how to lose: gallantly, graciously and without tantrums or tears. Hmm, I think. For me and my hierarchy-hungry trio this could be easier said than done.

Because I wonder whether their 'be-first' focus and subsequent fear of failure has been heightened by being one boy within a battalion of boys. I wonder whether their competitive spirit is actually stronger than that of other people's sons, or whether that is merely my perception as I am bombarded by three, and not just one or even two, competitive boy bust-ups.

I compare and contrast my own parents' gender-heavy upbringings to add to my rigorously empirical research.

My father, one of four boys, adopted the 'you snooze, you lose' approach to life in general, and to the dinner table in particular. 'If you didn't grab it first, someone else surely would!' he remembers, ladling a second helping of roast potatoes on to his already full plate. Survival, in his male household, of the fittest and the fastest. The competitive urge at its testosterone-fuelled best.

My mother, by contrast, one of five girls and a boarding-school boy, lived a more solicitous oestrogen-influenced life. 'FHB,' she pleads now, at each and every supper-table scrum. 'Family Hold Back . . . and you should never be the one to eat the very last slice,' she explains – in vain. I give my fellow female a sympathetic smile, put the serving spoon down and we watch, resigned, as our men tuck in.

Extreme MOB adds fuel to my fact-finding fire.

'Competitive? You bet! My boys can make a competition of just about anything! The longest wee, the loudest burp, even who can wobble their loose tooth worst! Sometimes, it can help get things done – like getting ready for school – but I do occasionally wonder whether it might be nice if they did as I ask because I'm asking them to, and *not* because they want to win!'

I nod with all-too-acute understanding, and turn to Singleson MOB. She nods too, although I sense that her pain is a tad less intense.

'We have to time our son to get him to tidy his room,' she agrees. 'No stop watch, no incentive . . . no can do. But I have to admit, it works every time!'

While it seems that being a multiple MOB may exacerbate the issue, solo sons are far from immune to the 'be-first' fixation.

So now, in the aftermath of the party, and with tent taken down, I have time to ponder the wise – but possibly worrying – words of fellow MOBs.

Have the FOB and I, like my MOB mates, also fanned the flames of competitiveness in our already overzealous battalion of boys? Have we used their natural competitive spirit to achieve our own, albeit well-intentioned, ends?

I start my deliberations with the subject closest to their hearts and thus most on my mind: food.

Like many twenty-first-century parents, I belong to the 'Jamie' generation. A generation that is fixated on five-a-day, which eschews ready meals and bakes its own bread.

And so, from the moment my babies shun breast for banana, I mush, mulch and mince with the determination and devotion of a truffle-seeking sow. I steam sweet potatoes (much healthier than boiling) and bake my own breadsticks (more flavour, less salt). With one eye on the vitamins, the other on the fat, I make meals in ice cubes and slop purée in pots before chuffing, cooing and cajoling my health-giving gunk into the mouths – mostly open – of my infant sons.

And when tooting like a train doesn't get them to eat up their greens, I adopt the 'king-of-the-castle' competitive approach.

'Oooh,' I say, spearing a sprout with my smallest son's fork, 'Sensible Son has nearly cleared *his* plate . . .' Feisty Fellow leans across the table to look at the offending object. 'I bet you can't clear yours before he does.' Feisty Fellow stuffs the sprout in his mouth and, like a man possessed, prongs another.

'Well done!' I say next, giving number-two son my fullest attention. 'You've eaten all your peas.' Grinning, he basks in my maternal gaze. I turn to his still-struggling older sibling. 'Look – Binary Boy's eaten his all up . . . *and* he's younger than you!' Shooting his brother a Horrid Henry glare, Sensible Son pounces like a panther on his remaining petits pois. They scatter like acorns under the table; the unfortunate few make it into his mouth.

'Wow, you were super quick with your sprouts . . .' I say, positively stroking my smallest son. 'Now . . . let's see if your middle brother can eat all his chicken before . . . before I count to . . . how old are you again, Feisty Fellow?'

'I'm four, nearly – *much* older than Best Boy Friend. He's still only three,' he splutters, mouth full of mash.

I let that one pass. 'OK. Four then. One . . . two . . . two and a quarter . . .'

Suddenly, all three join in with this implied race for recognition, clattering forks and scraping plates.

'I won!' Sensible Son pants.

'No you didn't,' squeals Binary Boy. 'You cheated! Half of your chicken is on the floor, you haven't eaten *any* of your sprouts. And anyway, you didn't have as much as me in the first place!'

'Did too . . .' retorts my biggest boy. 'Can't help it if I'm a faster eater 'n you, can I? *And* – even if we're racing – I don't like sprouts!'

Ignoring the Brussels debate, I interject – once again, reception-teacher-in-training. 'Erm, eating fast is not *necessarily* a good thing. You should slow down, savour your food, enjoy it.'

For a moment, the boys cease their squabbling. Look at me like a misplaced Martian.

'But you timed us, you counted . . .' Sensible Son quite rightly protests.

'*And* you said, "Wow, that was quick!"' affirms his younger brother. Nothing like a common enemy to bond the brotherhood.

Feisty Fellow, oblivious to the argument, finishes ploughing through his plate and lets out a volcanic burp. 'Done!' he announces amid approval from his brothers for his record-breaking belch. 'What's for pud?'

With my eye now firmly fixed on post-bedtime wine, I take the custard off the cooker and ladle it, carefully and equally, into their bowls.

Unsurprisingly perhaps, and unlike the first course, there is no need to time this custard contest. Still.

'He had more custard than me!' whines Binary Boy seconds later, eyeing his still-eating sibling. I shoot him a 'Don't-even-go-there' glare and try to scoot him upstairs for a bath.

'I'm not dirty!' he attempts.

'If you go now, you can get in first . . .' I tempt, realising, fractionally too late, the inevitably disastrous effect of this reason to race. Sensible Son and Feisty Fellow leap from their chairs, hot on their brother's custard-heavy heels.

'I wanna be first too!' they thunder, racing up the stairs and violently vying for pole plug-free position. Feisty Fellow is trampled underfoot.

'For pity's sake . . .' I mutter under end-of-the-day breath. I scale the stairs, shepherd my disparate herd to the bath and thence, thankfully – and significantly more calmly – to bed.

An hour later, wine glass in grateful hand, I reflect on the evening's events. The manuals have painted only part of the picture. Yes, competition is healthy for boys; can encourage and inspire. And yes, your lad should learn to be gracious in defeat. What they fail to point out, however, is that if *you*, as the parent, overuse this testosterone technique, losing a boy battle may result in a riot, *their* tantrums, *your* tears.

More recently, as the boys grow in both stature and sophistication, it is obvious that merely the incentive of gaining the metaphorical, and often literal, upper hand is not enough.

I try adopting the simple 'want-to-win' approach. We are in the post-extension garden, clearing yet another patch of ex-temporary skip ground.

'Boys,' I shout, 'can you help me, please? Can you each pick up ten mouldy apples and put them in the compost bin?'

Sensible Son looks at me, doesn't move.

'Will you time me?' he asks.

'No,' I say, 'I don't have a watch. Come on. Let's see who can do it fastest – you or your brothers . . .'

He looks at me again, cocks his mock-teenage head to one side.

'What'll you give me if I do?' he asks.

'Oh, for goodness sake!' I huff. 'Look, you can have my eternal gratitude,' I promise, 'and a big fat kiss!'

A look of sheer horror at the prospect of this unsolicited affection flits across his face and he sets off abruptly in the opposite direction. Meanwhile, his younger brothers set – more than willingly – to 'me-first' work.

Thereafter, therefore, we employ more subtle strategies to encourage co-operation in our, too-quickly-maturing – yet still mini- – man.

'Hey, look at this!' I say to him, gesturing towards a particularly alarming box of sugar-packed cereal. 'Each helping contains nearly twenty-nine per cent of your recommended daily intake of sugar!'

He examines the data with the absolute interest of a facts-and-figures-obsessed boy. 'Cor, you're right, Mum,' he says. 'And look at the salt content . . . that's appalling. The others can eat that if they want to, but I'm having porridge for breakfast today!'

'Good idea,' I say, pleased that he's come to his own healthy conclusion. No longer competing just with his siblings, but more importantly perhaps, with, and *for*, himself.

But there are unexpected downsides to increasing his awareness.

'I'm not sure you want to be eating that, Mum,' he says, scrutinising the generous blob of mayo I'm dolloping on my bread.

'Here . . . look . . . if you have that *and* cheese, you'll have eaten more fat than you're actually allowed in a week!'

'Gee, thanks for that,' I accede, before reluctantly removing the saturated spread.

And thus the evidence stacks up against me.

I will accept that in my capacity as a MOB, I *have* embraced, and even at times abused, my sons' competitive instincts to encourage them to eat more healthily, run faster, reach higher, excel. To get into the bath, out the door, to put on their shoes.

So, in that respect, yes, your Honour, I plead guilty to having fanned their competitive flames.

But what I struggle to see is that I lit their fire in the first place.

Because that fire was surely lit when the boys were born 'boy'. Teeming with testosterone, programmed to push. From the moment they hit the ground – running – I firmly believe they were ready to race.

'Should he be doing that?' I remember a MOG friend asking me way back when, eyeing a fifteen-month-old Feisty Fellow, as he prepared to launch himself down an exceptionally scary slide.

'Probably not,' I acknowledged, 'but you try stopping him!'

With a blood-curdling whoop, he skedaddled to the bottom, before racing – as always – to catch up with his brothers.

Manual six states that you have to re-present foods to fussy eaters sixteen (or was it seventeen?) times before you finally admit defeat. So on Sunday, in addition to the customary carrots and peas, we have sprouts.

'Oh go on . . .' I wheedle. 'Just one tiny bite . . . they're not going to kill you!'

Sensible Son shakes his head. 'I've told you before and I'll tell you again: I DON'T LIKE SPROUTS!'

'Your brothers have eaten all theirs . . .'

He eyes me with disdain.

'Did you know that sprouts contain more vitamins than any other veg? That they're a super food?'

He yawns.

'If you eat that sprout, I'll give you some sweets . . .'

His mouth stays resolutely shut.

'Mum,' he says Lola-looking me straight in the eye, 'I will not EVER, NEVER, eat a Brussels sprout. Understood? Well,' he adds slyly, 'not unless you come into the chicken coop with me next time we're at Good-life Gran's and PICK UP a chicken . . .'

His bird-phobic mother shudders, picks up his sprout-laden plate and takes it to the bin.

He smiles his winning smile. Two can play at that game, I can almost sense him saying. Check, mate.

Later that evening, my Big Brother calls. I recount the long-standing sprout stand-off with a mixture of despair and delight. Despair that I will have to up the competitive stakes to achieve my aims; delight that my savvy son is learning to turn the tables.

He laughs, loudly.

'What's so funny?' I ask, ever the sensitive little sister.

'Well, this competition thing your boys have . . . it's just so . . . so *you*, isn't it? I mean, if we had a fourth child, would you have a fifth?'

I sit, stunned at the suggestion that I could be anywhere near as competitive as my alpha-male offspring. It's being boys which makes them want to win, isn't it? And I'm different . . . I'm a *girl*.

'Of course not!'

I laugh shakily. Perhaps it's more than chromosomes that cut your competitive cloth. Not just about whether you wear boxers or a bra. Maybe, I allow, albeit reluctantly, it's got more to do with the cut of . . . your genes.

Five wicked ways to exploit the 'me-first' mentality

- You can get your sons to eat almost anything by telling them that whoever eats quickest/most/best wins. Anything, that is, except Brussels sprouts.
- Invest in a stopwatch (must be digital, analogue's not accurate enough), then time them to clean their room/your room/the house. Know, however, that you'll need to go straight to the supermarket and purchase more polish.
- Tell them that whoever gets in the bath first won't have to sit next to the plug. (Be prepared to be trampled underfoot in the ensuing up-the-stairs scrum.)
- Inform your son sweetly that 'When he was your age, your older brother could spell *all* his Key Stage 1 words.' Harsh, but helpful.
- Use the 'Who-can-wee-loudest-and-longest?' competition to eke out necessary pre-bedtime pees. (Then remind the FOB he's too big to take part.)

A Mystery à la Blyton for a Bevy of Boys

Chapter 1: In which Sensible Son makes a shocking discovery . . .

'I can't believe it's the end of the hols already!' said Sensible Son.

'I know,' agreed Tom. 'It feels like we've only just broken up and yet we've had six whole weeks of school-free frolics!'

Dick grinned. 'Camping . . . swimming . . . sailing . . . surfing . . .'

'And ice creams!' added Binary Boy, licking his lips. 'Don't forget the ice creams.'

'Weren't they wizard!' agreed Feisty Fellow. 'Simply spiffing!' He made short work of an imaginary ice cream with his oversized tongue.

Everyone chortled happily without a care in the world. It was a glorious September day: sparkling sunshine with just the slightest of chills, to remind you that autumn was right around the bend. Indeed, the leaves on the trees had just started to turn golden brown; it would be conker time soon. Hip hip hurrah!

'What shall we do today?' asked Tom. 'The day's too smashing to waste!'

'How about a bicycle ride?' suggested Harry. 'I can pop home over the fields to get mine. Mum could make us all a picnic and we can bike up to the lake.'

'Great idea!' chorused everyone. 'Your mum's picnics are always absolutely top notch – homemade Scotch eggs, hand-reared sausage rolls and lashings and lashings of just-grated ginger beer!'

'Right then,' organised Sensible Son. 'I'll just get Dad to fix my brakes quickly – they're ever so unattractively squeaky – and then we'll all meet back here at five p.m. sharp.' His fellow adventurers nodded their agreement and prepared to speed off. 'Oh, and make sure you bring extra emergency rations . . . just in case!'

A bevy of boys set off in all directions, promising to return for five p.m. prompt. A bicycle ride *and* a picnic – how utterly unimaginable, two treats in one day!

The boys met at five p.m. sharp. Everyone was grinning excitedly. Everyone, that is, except . . .Sensible Son.

'I can't find my bicycle!' said Sensible Son, dismally. 'I've looked absolutely everywhere and it's just vanished into thin air.'

'Well, if you've looked everywhere, then there's only one explanation. Sensible Son,' said Dick, solemnly, 'your bicycle's been . . . STOLEN!'

The boys gasped and then nodded. There was only one thing for it.

If their friend's bicycle had been stolen, then it was up to them to help solve the mystery. Armed with only a shortage of clues and an out-of-date map, they would work together to find Sensible Son's bicycle and, even more importantly, to catch the THIEF!

Well, what did I expect? I did marry a male

Our sun-scorched eyes met across a never-ending beach on the south-western shores of the Mediterranean. The embers of a camp fire smouldered romantically behind me as I gazed in unconcealed awe at the Greek God who stood, colossus-like, in front of me; an abundance of carbon curls and long, lean limbs. I was a quivering nineteen, the future Father of Boys just a year or so younger.

Wordlessly, he turned towards me. With well-honed, bronzed fingers he slowly and sensuously unzipped his shorts. I held my breath.

And then, with a devilish grin, he employed his anatomy to try to put out the flames of both the fire on the beach and that which had been burning bright in my freshly besotted belly.

The mass of now sodden embers died a nauseously putrid death; my passion – for the fireman and for the better, or indeed the worse – did not.

Seventeen years later. I am, as so often, standing at the sink. Washing up and making the most of a moment on my own to listen to *Woman's Hour* without any squawking, squealing or burping of bums. Suddenly, the previously loud, but largely harmless, hilarity – commonplace when the boys are doing . . . well, pretty much anything, with their father – is replaced by a shriek of such magnitude that even this impervious MOB looks up from yet another cereal-encrusted bowl.

Four boys, large and small, are huddled round a fire in the

corner of the field. The biggest 'boy' (aka the FOB) holds a long, burning stick in his hands. The slightly smaller version we know as Sensible Son has his trousers round his knees and is taking aim at said burning stick. Binary Boy and Feisty Fellow are gleefully spellbound, watching events.

'What on earth do you think you're doing?' I yell through the open window, mainly at my husband, but I suspect the rest of the village may well catch my drift.

'We're experimenting, Mum,' Sensible Son shouts back. 'Dad's teaching us about the power of fire, so's we can learn to be safe!'

I question this distinctly dubious logic and glare at my glowing husband.

Is it the fire, I wonder, or the excitement of a small child trapped in the body of a grown man that is making him flush?

'Not like that, you're not!' I retort, pulling both age and wisdom rank. 'And,' I tell my now deflated other half, '*you* should know better!'

'Sorry, Muuumm,' chant four identikit voices, pulling up pants and downing sticks.

'I should think so too!' I huff pompously, resuming my painstaking removal of a particularly determined wodge of Weetabix. 'I should think so too!'

Perhaps I should've paid attention in biology, rather than making eyes at the dentist's son.

My husband, my beloved FOB: one of two boys (albeit followed by a miraculous go-getter girl). His father: one of three boys. His father's father: also one of a multitude of males. And it is, so I have been post-education informed (and as I frequently take pains to remind my man) the paternal – not maternal – genetic history which influences the sex of a couple's future progeny. That'll teach me for not listening.

174

Or it would, if I regretted for one moment being what I am now: a proud and happy – if somewhat frazzled and frequently perplexed – mother of three small boys, and wife of one larger maxi-man.

Which, of course, I don't.

But my 'serial bridesmaid' status (always the MOB and never a MOG) should, therefore, come as no surprise. Nor indeed should I be shocked by my husband's testosterone talents.

For the FOB is, quite frankly, as bad (or as good, depending on who's talking and the time of the month) as any of the *genuinely* young male members of our family.

While at work (I have been reliably informed) my husband maintains a dignity and decorum befitting his role, at home he reveals the boy-blue colours of his officially golden epaulets. At home, stripped of rank and responsibility, he joyously joins 'the pack' and becomes easily as excitable, absolutely as competitive, totally as tumultuous as his sons.

The only difference is that being over eighteen and (in the eyes of the law, if not always his wife) an adult, *he* gets to decide when to go to A&E and not me.

Case in point.

Learning the lessons of long-distance travel disasters, we spend our summer holiday camping in Cornwall. A tent the size of a small marquee, a boot packed to the brim with bangers and beans, a roofbox fit to burst with surfboards and spades. Boy Bliss.

It's a rare *Famous Five* day: azure blue skies, a searing sun and the faintest hint of a refreshing breeze. The perfect day for an expedition.

Sensible Son takes the lead, as he so often does. 'Dad can be Julian, cos he's eldest boy and I'll be Dick!' he declares.

'Then I'll be George – she's a tomboy anyway,' agrees a suspiciously accommodating Binary Boy. 'And you can be

Anne,' he adds, nodding towards Feisty Fellow, 'cos you do look like a girl!'

'I's not a girl, is I, Mummy?' shrieks our youngest, brushing his uncut mop from over his eyes.

Here we go again.

'No of course you're not!' I shoot his too-canny brother what I hope is a suitably 'cross-Mum' look. 'I know . . . why don't you be Timmy – you love dogs. You get to leap about and dogs *definitely* deserve a treat!'

Mollified, he begins to pant, picks up a stick with his teeth and sniffs my bottom. Maybe this isn't such a great idea.

Still.

'I guess that makes me Anne . . . again,' I grump. I make it clear that I do not intend to pass on Blyton's sexual typecasting to yet another generation of males. 'So, I'll sort out the kit, shall I, while *Julian* finishes the washing-up?'

We set off von Trapp-style along the coastal path, fields to the left, hedge to the right. The boys hurtle up the hill, terriers after a rabbit, and I take the FOB's hand happily in mine. At this rate, we might even be able to hold a conversation.

As we reach the top of the 'mountain', we pause to catch our breath and the stunning view: fishing boats hug the sides of a meandering creek; an enclave of pine trees perches precariously on the cliff edge; impossibly lush grass stretches endlessly down to a sparkling sea.

'Wow!' I puff, looking round for my husband and hoping that he will share in my appreciation of this veritable Cornish feast.

But the FOB has gone.

Vamooshed.

I turn 360 degrees, puzzled by his sudden disappearance. Maybe he's gone to answer a call of nature, I think.

Or maybe not.

Squinting against the sun, I can just about make out what can only be my Greek God hurtling, out of control, down the grassy slopes towards the water below. Arms stretched wide, he both looks and sounds like a World War Two bomber.

'Neeeooowwww,' he shrieks, much to the delight of our enthusiastic, if slightly bemused, boys. Carried away by the self-same exuberance that has given rise to their father's strange behaviour, they decide to join in.

'Neeeeoowww!' scream all four, flying skilfully and speedily over the rough, tough terrain.

'Neee . . . OWWWW!'

Suddenly – silence.

My biggest boy, my Spitfire, has been shot down, mid-flight, by a strategically placed cowpat. With slapstick precision, he has skidded into the humming hillock, performed a fairly impressive (for someone oh-so-terribly tall) forward roll and landed in an undignified – and presumably smelly – heap, on the far side of the slope.

I hold my breath as our sons race to their beloved father's side to check that he's still alive. He raises a reassuring arm.

'Don't worry . . . I'm fine!' he shouts.

Relieved that we won't have to try to summon an air ambulance to this most remote of coverage-free spots, I adopt an overly responsible response to my 'child's' bonkers behaviour.

'What on earth did you think you were doing?' I remonstrate with uncanny echoes of the pee-stick saga.

'Sorry, Muummm!' he retorts once again, flashing his still devilish grin and surreptitiously rubbing his right-handed wrist.

'I should think so too!' I sniff.

And then, because I can't help myself any more than he could, I laugh and I laugh until the tears roll down my wrinkles and my chortling cheeks can't take any more.

Ten minutes later, we peel off the poo, pick up our rucksacks and set off once more on our exploratory adventure. Miraculously, we make it back to the car without further mishap.

'Why don't you drive us to the beach?' suggests the FOB.

I eye him suspiciously. *Him* suggesting *I* drive? 'OK,' I say, catching the keys.

I park the car tight in to the hedge by the path leading to the afternoon's chosen sandy spot. The boys tumble out of the back like overly squished sardines. Meanwhile, the FOB pops open the roofbox and rummages inside.

'Body boards – three; buckets – three; spades – three; *my* spade – one; wetsuits . . .' The list of equipment goes on. And on.

'Hang on,' I interrupt. '*My* spade? What's this *my* spade business?'

While his odour is still distinctly bovine, he suddenly looks just a little bit sheepish. 'I . . . I packed my own spade, you know – the metal garden one, just in case . . .'

In case? In case what? We had a sudden summer snow storm and needed to dig ourselves out? There were no toilets at the campsite and we needed to improvise?

'No wonder the car was so full on the journey down!' I explode, the memory of sitting in interminable traffic jams packed between camping mats and mallets still painfully embedded on the backs of my knees.

He slings the spade over his shoulder and lollops off towards the beach. The boys have raced on ahead and are already halfway down the many sea-going steps. I pick up the picnic, scowl at *that* spade and trot along, disgruntled, behind.

I have encountered many phenomena in my life as a MOB.

Spade envy, however, is a new one on me.

Despite my anti-Anne feminist pretensions, I happily set up camp on the sand while the boys go off and do, well, boys' things. Things that I have no interest in doing and, quite frankly, don't understand.

Take dam building, for instance. Hour upon hour spent lugging huge boulders from spot A to spot B, in the hope of creating a piddling pool which will be destroyed within a few tidal moments of its sweat-inducing completion. If indeed you manage to finish it and aren't overtaken instead by the weather, the water or a random small child who insists on removing your rocks just as quickly as you can put them in place. What on earth, ask me and my MOB mind, can possibly be the point?

Today's beach is, however, apparently not endowed with the requisite characteristics for successful damming, and so the men in my life embark instead on another of their favourite pointless pastimes. The digging of holes.

I watch, with female fascination, as they plan their project. Step one: pick your spot. (The choice of the correct site is, for reasons that are not immediately – or ever – apparent, critical.) Step two: assemble your excavation team, biggest on the inside, smallest on the out. Step three: take up tools and begin to dig.

All very organised, all well and good, but *why*?

Some thirty seconds after dig-off, Binary Boy inadvertently sprays sand in his younger brother's soon-streaming eyes. Sensible Son stubs his bare toe on his (thankfully) plastic spade. And the army of sand-Scoops are dropping like flies.

Sensing that I am not about to budge from my picnic-preparing base camp to deal with his troop of wounded soldiers, the FOB sorts out his junior JCBs, before attacking the ground again with vigour and verve.

'Come on, chaps!' he enthuses. 'Put your backs into it!'

One by one, my sons run out of both energy and enthusiasm

for their hole-digging duties and join me instead for their fix of food. This, at least, is one male obsession I *can* comprehend.

Like the Lone Ranger, my husband, however, gallops ever on, totally focused on achieving his goal. Whatever happens, however much his right wrist, I now note absent-mindedly, appears to be irritating him, he *will* dig that hole. And it will be bigger and it will be deeper than any other hole on this beach, if not the entire Roseland Peninsula. Here and now, that hole, to him, is . . . everything.

Gradually, we lose sight of him: first his legs disappear, followed rapidly by his torso and then his arms, until all that remains of my dearly beloved is his ever-so-slightly balding and ever-so-slowly burning head.

The boys lose interest in their increasingly absent father, and head for the waves.

I pick up my book.

When I look up some two minutes later, even his head has gone. And from where I am sitting, my husband has been replaced by four or five other FOB clones: middle-aged men, clasping the hands of their small sons as they gaze with expressions ranging from overt awe to outright envy into the now cavernous black hole.

'Look at the size of that!' says Clone One, breathless with excitement.

'Wish I'd thought of that!' adds Clone Two, wistfully.

'His is much, *much* bigger than yours, Daddy!' points out Clone One's little lad, earning an Eeyore eyeful from his crestfallen FOB.

At this moment, my own mammoth meercat pops up his now glowing scalp from the back of beyond. He grins at his audience and brandishes the focus of their fervour for all to ogle and admire.

'Oh, this old spade . . . I just threw it in at the last moment. After all, you never know!'

Fellow FOBs nod appreciatively and murmur their agreement. 'Absolutely!' they concur as they reluctantly disband, heading, heads down, back to their own MOB-manned base camps and their paltry plastic spades.

Seconds later, a MOB army unites in one voice the length and breadth of the beach: 'You needn't think *you're* bringing one of *those* next year!'

'Sorry,' I mouth, lifting my shoulders with a 'Well-what-can-one-do?' shrug. 'Sorry!'

The FOB, meanwhile, continues to dig.

Later on, as the sun sinks low over the emerald-green sea, we head to the steps for the long climb back to the car. Halfway up, I pause for breath. I am, of course, carrying an exhausted Feisty Fellow, as his father has his one working hand full with his spade. I look down at the suddenly almost-empty beach.

Clone One is racing his son across the sand.

'You can't catch me!' I hear him taunt his obviously shattered, now wailing opponent. And then I watch – horrified – as he hurtles headlong into my husband's coveted chasm.

His wife stands at the brink and peers into the void. 'What on earth do you think you're doing?' she screams at her presumably embarrassed, but uninjured, FOB.

I grin. It's nice to know sometimes that I'm not alone.

Back at the campsite, our sun-blasted boys have been swiftly showered, removing at best the uppermost crust from their salty skins. Dressed in pirate pyjamas and snuggly socks, they are now suffering from two of the worst afflictions known to MOB. They are tired, and they are hungry.

'Is supper ready yet, Mum?' they whine. 'We're starvin'!'

I think about telling them for the umpteenth time that they are extremely fortunate compared to the many children in this world who are indeed starving . . . and then think better of it. Ancient though I am, I can still remember what it feels like to be six, shattered and, yes, starving, after an endless day on a sun-sapping beach.

'Nearly,' I reply, willing the pasta to boil just a smidgen faster above the flickering flame. 'Why don't you ask Dad to play a game with you before supper?'

The FOB raises a semi-reluctant eyebrow, but realises that there is, in these canvas confines, no chance of escape. He puts down the newspaper he has just picked up for, admittedly, the first time this holiday, and picks up instead a deck of cards.

'OK, who wants to play pairs?' Like premenstrual mums around a full tin of truffles, they huddle in close to their dealer dad.

Fifteen minutes later, the pasta is cooked.

'Supper's ready!' I shout, poking my head into the tent.

'Just coming . . .' says the FOB. 'Well done, guys – good game! Right, let's go and have supper now.'

'Team hug first!' demands an allegedly famished Binary Boy, grabbing his father's long legs round about the height of his knees.

'Yes, team hug, team hug!' chant his brothers in unison, jumping up and down with an energy that appeared to have abandoned them earlier on during the slog up the steps.

'OK, come on then . . . team hug!' I roll my eyes and leave them to it.

Perhaps I should explain. The 'team hug' is the fault, I think, of manual number four. Or maybe it was five? Anyway. It was invented by the FOB in response to my assertion that he should adopt a more 'hands-on' approach to his still-small sons.

'It says here that it's really important for the male role model to be physical with his boys, to demonstrate tenderness . . . apparently, sons learn empathy largely from their fathers.' I look up. 'Are you listening?' I ask, unconvinced by the way he appears to be focusing more on *Grand Designs* than on my emotional advice.

'Listening? Absolutely,' he replies, with irritatingly accurate fluency. 'You want me to be more, er . . . physical with the boys . . . I'll teach them how to rugby tackle this weekend shall I? They'll love that!'

I groan. 'Not that kind of physical. Cuddles, kisses . . . you know – "gentle" physical.'

He looks at me, blankly. A Bonny–Clyde moment.

'But I kiss them at bedtime. And when I leave on a Monday to go to work for the week. And I gave Feisty Fellow a cuddle when he, er . . . fell off his bike, remember?' I stare at him, without a word. 'OK, OK. So I could probably be a *bit* more "touchy feely" . . . I'll try . . .' His gaze slides stealthily back to a particularly impressive roof structure. 'I promise!'

And so it was that the boy-bonding 'team hug' was born.

From the outside, it looks and sounds like a squealing plethora of under-fed pigs. Assorted unidentifiable limbs bulge and blight the straining sides of the tent, bellows and belches (bottom and otherwise) abound. I begin my silent count . . . one, two, three. By ten, there'll be moaning: 'It's my turn to sit on Dad'; by twenty, there'll be shouting: 'Ow . . . get off my head!'; by thirty, there'll be tears: 'He hit me on purpose!'

This time, I make it to seventeen.

'Right, that's enough. Stop now, boys, calm down,' pleads

the FOB, trying – in vain – to extricate himself from the clutches of his now predictably overexcited and out-of-control crew. 'Ow – let go of my wrist! I said . . . THAT'S ENOUGH!'

I wade into the sty and put an arm around the heaving shoulders of a whacked Feisty Fellow. Gently, I lead my sweaty – and now suddenly subdued – children to the dinner table. Their 'male moment' has definitely been 'touchy', certainly 'feely', but somehow is not *quite* what I'd had in mind.

'Why don't you be "Mum" and dish out the pasta?' I suggest brightly, handing my deflated husband a ladle. He delves into the saucepan and winces.

'What's up?' I ask.

'Nothing,' he grimaces, smiling weakly.

'Doesn't look like nothing to me!' I sigh. 'Do you think you should go and get it checked out?'

The FOB shakes his head and resumes piling on the pasta. 'I'm fine,' he says, 'honestly. You fuss too much.'

It's the following spring before he decides, finally, to casually confess.

The FOB is in the garden, practising a particularly complicated morris dance move in anticipation of his annual appearance at the local village fete. The move involves, to my untrained eye, lots of shouting, loads of leaping and the un-coordinated juggling of two very large sticks. Again: utterly incomprehensible boy bliss.

'You know . . . I think I might . . . just . . . have . . . um . . . broken something when I fell over!' he puffs, as he grapples with the complexities of doing two things at once. A stick clatters to the ground, narrowly missing his toe.

I scour my mental accident case file for incidents involving my largest lad and falling over, and draw a blank.

'Fall over? When did you fall over?'

'You know . . .' he mumbles. 'Cornwall . . . the cowpat . . . my accident.'

'Oh, that "*accident*",' I say, hiding an unhelpful grin behind a dirty gardening glove. I'm tempted, oh so tempted, to waggle my finger at my hapless husband, to remonstrate, reproach, remind him that I had indeed suggested at the time that a trip to the hospital might have been in order.

But I don't.

After all, the FOB is my husband – not a Morris *Minor* like his sons, but a full-blown Morris *Man*, capable of making his own decisions. His own mistakes. And maybe, even, learning from them.

Glancing at his watch, he dons his hat, picks up his bells and careers down the path to meet his fellow morris majors.

'Be careful!' I warn automatically, as he speeds down the track, scattering gravel and grime. There's an ominous thud followed by an inaudible string of expletives. I sigh and head indoors to start on supper.

'I am his wife, not his mother,' I say to the stove. The FOB is a big boy now. *Surely* he can take care of himself, can't he?

I look up 'Doctor's surgery' and pick up the phone.

Ten places you'll never find your FOB

- Cleaning the loo/sink/shower.
- Using the wash basket/washing machine/washing line.
- *Emptying* the Hoover.
- Winding things down when it's high time for bed.
- Buying cards and presents for sons' friends' parties. Actually, that should read, buying cards and presents for anyone, full stop. Even if they are *his* godchildren.
- Writing a menu for the week.
- Telling the boys that 'pull my finger' is not an appropriate instruction at the dining-room table.
- Doing Hama beads.
- Flicking through the kids' clothes catalogue for next season's shorts.
- Sorting out the Tupperware.

So what kind of Father is your FOB?
The FOB Quick Quiz Test

1. Your wife is about to give birth. What words do you whisper in her adorable ear?
    a) 'You're doing wonderfully, my angel . . . I couldn't do better!'
    b) 'Does this button switch your Tens machine off or on?'
    c) 'I think you've had quite enough gas and air!'
    d) None of the above. Why on earth would I want to be present at the birth?

2. Your newborn son is placed in your arms. Do you say:
    a) 'He's absolutely amazing!' with tears in your eyes.
    b) 'Should his head really be flopping back like that?'
    c) 'Is his Apgar score up to scratch? I trust my boy is a perfect ten.'
    d) In my arms . . . not likely while he's covered in that gunk!

3. It's 3 a.m. and you can vaguely hear your baby crying. Do you:
    a) Leap out of bed and warm up a bottle, patting the duvet down thoughtfully as you go.
    b) Throw a book out of the window at what must surely be next door's mad moggy.
    c) Switch on the lights, consult your clock and inform your sleeping partner that your intelligent offspring is bang on time for her breast.
    d) Baby . . . what baby? Surely you don't expect me to hear the baby from the spare room?

4. Your son's first word is 'Mum'. How do you react?

   a) Say, 'That's absolutely fitting, given all the time *you've* dedicated to raising *our* son.'

   b) Chortle incredulously, 'Did he just say "bum"?'

   c) Frown: 'I'm sure he should be blending his phonemes by now,' and immediately embark on remedial phonics.

   d) Grunt from your hotel room: 'He never says anything to me on the phone.'

5. You take your boy to play in the park. You meet up with fellow FOBs. You vaguely notice that your son is dangling by one arm from the back of the slide. What do you do?

   a) Interrupt your conversation and rush to his aid.

   b) Mumble, 'Goodness, that looks painful!' and carry on your chat.

   c) See this as the perfect opportunity for experiential learning.

   d) I can't be expected to do two things at once, can I? Anyone would think I have eyes in the back of my head!

6. Your son is sitting at the dinner table, trumping for Britain. Your wife is telling him that he really should stop. Do you say:

   a) 'Your mother is right and she should be revered.'

   b) 'Better out than in, lad,' and do one yourself.

   c) 'That is unacceptable behaviour . . . go and sit on The Step.'

   d) 'Are there seconds of spaghetti? I'm absolutely famished!'

7. Your school-age son comes home to tell you he's bottom of the class. He's upset. How do you respond?

   a) Sit down calmly with his homework and help him improve.

   b) Advise him that if he copies his best mate, he'll do better next time.

c) Call a home tutor.

d) He's at school already? How time flies.

8. It's Christmas and you and your family are attending a church service. Everyone else is singing carols. Your boy is shooting the congregation with a Stickle Brick gun. How do you react?

    a) Slip unnoticed from your pew and bring your son home to roost. Join in together with 'no crib for a bed'.

    b) Make a gun with your finger and shoot the bugger back.

    c) Get the vicar's attention and point out your miscreant male. Some old-fashioned humiliation never did you any harm.

    d) 'Oooh, I love a good sing-song . . . don't you?'

If you answered mostly as: you are MYTHICAL FOB.
You are too good to be true. Have I met you? Are you married?

If you answered mostly bs: you are NATURAL FOB.
Being a FOB comes naturally to you. Too naturally. Maybe you should be helping your partner, instead of pinching your boy's toys?

If you answered mostly cs: you are AMBITIOUS FOB.
You should definitely stop reading my mothering manuals. Cut the kid some slack . . . and let him be a boy.

If you answered mostly ds: you are ABSENT FOB.
It takes two to tango and childhood doesn't last long. Perhaps you could try being just a little more hands-on?

If you can't beat 'em, join 'em

So. I didn't ask to be a MOB.

I wanted – and was fortunate enough – to become a mum.

But now, here I am, a mother . . . of boys. A woman, who lives – day in, day out – the lives of her lads. Lives which are not always entirely in tune with my womanly expectations or wants. Lives which can leave me feeling, at times, like a female fish out of masculine water.

Over time, however, and with the benefit of reflection, research and not a little wine, I have come to accept the inevitable realities of my gender lot in life. I'd go further. I have come to embrace and even *enjoy* the experiences and exploits of my boy-bound world. I have moved from unsuspecting female floundering among sons to comfortable and conversant mother of boys.

Discovering, and appreciating, the 'beautiful game' (although I still wouldn't go that far) is just one revelation along the road to fully fledged MOB.

It's April. Sensible Son and Binary Boy are at school. The conversation between myself and my still-at-home son goes something like this:

'Mum . . .'

'Hmmm?' (Staring at the computer screen, randomly clicking on 'Pointless-Property-Perusing.com'.)

'Mummy . . .'

'Hmmmmm?' (Continuing to browse . . . you know, there really are some stunning soundproofed places out there!)

'MUMMEEE!'

'Yes,' (logging off P-cubed.com), 'what is it . . .' (shutting computer) ' . . . darling?' (turning to face small child.)

'I's gonna be a footballer when I's growned up!'

I resist the temptation to correct his four-year-old grammar. His teachers can tackle that one when he starts school in September.

'A footballer?' I repeat. He nods, emphatically, sending his Kevin Keegan curls into convulsions. 'OK . . .' I say slowly. 'But why?'

Despite living in a house with an abundance of anatomical balls, I have thus far managed to escape any obsessions with the more bouncy kind. The FOB has always preferred rowing to Rangers, while the male fascination for 'footie' appears to have gone over the heads of my two elder sons like a poorly placed penalty. And ever since I fell into a scrum-half's lap during a particularly sweaty circuits session at Bath University, it's rugby – for reasons which have little to do with balls – over Ronaldo for me. So Feisty Fellow's assertion comes as something of a – not entirely welcome – surprise.

'I'm gonna be rich!' he says, beaming. 'And famous!' I try to picture myself as a footballer's mum, dripping gold and glamour on the cover of *Hello!* – and fail. Nevertheless, I think, fingering his luscious locks, maybe I should put his long-awaited trip to the hairdressers on hold . . . just in case.

'Do you *really* want to play football?'

'I do, I do,' he chants, thrusting his knees high in the air. I smile at his enthusiasm and acknowledge that – unlike his trail-blazing brothers – he hasn't done any clubs of his very, very own.

I log back on to the laptop, looking this time not at houses, but for tots' football teams.

★ ★ ★

Kool Kickas, two weeks later.

I sit, bulging cheek by wobbly jowl, with a multitude of other MOBs, and the odd – very odd – overenthusiastic FOB. We crouch on pint-sized benches round the edge of the sports hall, staring resolutely into the middle distance like newly incarcerated inmates.

'What are *you* in for?' I'm tempted to ask the glum mum whose bottom overlaps so sociably with mine. 'Being a MOB,' she would answer, gesturing towards her acrylic-clad son, 'Total Looney' emblazoned on the back of his green and yellow shirt. 'You?' 'Same,' I would reply, indicating my own mini Maradona, scuttling about in an oversized T-shirt and big brother shorts. (The lessons I can just about cope with; buying the kit is taking this commitment to balls just a fraction too far.) She would nod in silent sympathy, shuffle her buttocks uncomfortably and refocus her glazed gaze on her soccer-loving son.

I grin conspiratorially to myself, imagining the conversations of the convicted afflicted. An out-of-control ball slaps against my shins, bringing me painfully back to the present, and I eye the clock hopefully. The big hand, let alone the little one, has barely moved.

Twenty minutes later, however, I've forgotten the time and forsaken the bench.

'Go, Feisty Fellow . . . go!' I shriek, jumping to my feet and jostling my previously numb bum against those of other equally excitable MOBs. 'Come on you greens . . . get the ball will you . . . *just kick it!*'

'Go reds!' retaliates the miserable MOB one up from me, cupping her hands in a homespun megaphone. I glare at her – The Opposition.

'Gre-eeens, gree-eeens!' I holler at the fragmented field of three- and four-year-olds.

A lanky lad – shouldn't he still be at school, or am I showing my age? – lollops over to the unruly audience.

'Can we keep it down a bit, ladies?' he asks politely. 'Let's let the little ones play, shall we? It *is* only a game!'

'Sorry, yes . . . sorry,' we mutter, hormonal hooligans, dropping awkwardly and somewhat embarrassed, on to our various bits of bench. 'Of course . . . of course, it's *only* a game.'

'Go reds!' whispers megaphone MOB.

'Gree-eens!' I hiss, fractionally louder.

The soccer tots, blissfully oblivious, play on.

As is our wont, Kindred MOB and I debate our various Damascus MOB moments, as our plethora of children play in the park.

'Do you think that we were always *meant* to be Mothers of Boys?' I cogitate, rolling a ball of Blu-Tack I've just found in my pocket. 'Not so high!' I shout at one son as he flies skywards on the swing.

'Maybe . . .' she says, eyeing her own testosterone trio affectionately as they career down the slide – backwards. 'I think you get what you can cope with in life. I don't think I could have done endless ballet or giggly girls, and Hannah Montana leaves me cold . . .' She breaks off as two of her sons leap on to her lap. 'I honestly believe,' she pants from under a bundle of coats, 'that I was destined to have a rumble-tumble of boys!'

To my surprise, her musings have some scientific substance.

A fellow MOB in Auckland, Dr Valerie Grant, found that women are indeed likely to produce the sex of children they're most naturally suited to bring up. ('Even', I reflect, recalling my original aversion to all things 'ball', 'even if that's not always immediately apparent to the mother herself!' Anyway.) According to Dr Grant, strong, dominant ladies have higher levels of testosterone and are more likely to give birth to typically more tumultuous sons. Add to this her research, which shows that a woman's testosterone-influenced egg may well have chosen which sex-bearing sperm it wishes to welcome *before* the sperm quite literally comes a'knocking, and you have an increasingly strong case for the suggestion that it's the woman, and not the man, who wears the sex-selection trousers.

Oh-kay.

So, on the downside, I will now have to admit to the FOB that it may be me, and not him, who is responsible after all for our shock of sons. *My* hormones, *my* eggs, it appears, and not *his* boy-bearing ancestors as I'd previously claimed, may hold the gender key.

But on the upside, my undoubtedly higher-than-average testosterone tally means that I now have an excuse for my less feminine foibles. Instead of being 'bossy', I can claim to be 'confident'. Less 'confrontational', more of a 'challenge'. No longer 'aggressive', but attractively 'assertive'.

'Que sera, sera', Grant seems to be saying – there's no point decrying your personal gender propensity. 'Consider yourself a specialist at your [particular] sex,' she advocates wisely, 'rather than yearning [unhelpfully and implausibly] for the other.'

And thus, in general, I do. I try to follow Grant's sensible advice. I endeavour to accept the blood and ballistics of my boy-heavy world, to embrace the mayhem and madness that are the inevitable outcome of living with a small army of men. I try, TRY, to avoid hankering forlornly after more instinctively girl-power pursuits.

But when I do spy even the faintest sparkle of 'girl' amid the incessant boy barrage, I swoop like an owl on a field full of mice.

My first furry victim is Sensible Son.

'Can we go into town, Mum?' he asks me one morning, out of the blue.

'Of course!' I say, gleefully. 'I'll just get my bag!'

Leaving his brothers with their father, we head for the High Street.

'Right – where to first?' I ask, excited by the extraordinary notion of window shopping with my son. 'Next? Monsoon? Fat Face?'

He gestures vaguely towards the top of town. 'GAME,' he replies. 'I really want to check out the latest Mario game for my DS.'

'Oh,' I say, swallowing my disappointment. I summon a smile, put away my purse and trot after my boy as he races up the road.

Next on the menu is Binary Boy.

'Mum, I want to sew something,' announces my artistic middle son another afternoon. 'Will you help me?'

'Sewing . . . oooh, I loved sewing when I was little. Of course I'll help you!' I empathise and enthuse. Heading happily for the nearest craft shop, I stock up on baskets of needles and tangles of thread, before, inspired by memories of my Mum-made presents, making him his very own sewing kit for Christmas.

To give him his due, he makes me a bag for my birthday. But from that female day forth, the kit has sat sadly behind his overflowing crate of lad-loved Lego, unused, abused and gathering dust.

Last on my prey list is Feisty Fellow.

'Can I 'elp you?' he asks one evening, sidling up to my legs as I cook yet another vat of stew.

'Absolutely,' I say eagerly, whooshing him on to the worktop at my be-aproned side. 'I'm always happy to have a helper in the kitchen!' He leans over the saucepan to sniff my mountain of meat.

'Is it chocolate?' he asks hopefully, licking his lips.

''Fraid not, no. It's stew – for supper,' I reply. 'You can peel me some potatoes, if you like?'

'No fanks,' he says politely. 'I fought it was chocolate!' Thus disappointed, he hops from his perch and sets off in search of a more appetising occupation.

Later, much later, I discover that I am not alone in sometimes adapting and even suppressing my natural preferences to suit my opposite-sex circumstances. This smothering of deep-held, even subconscious, instincts is, it appears, common not only to son-swamped MOBs, but also to their male counterparts: the girly-outnumbered Father of Girls: the FOGs. While we may live in different coloured houses, we share, apparently, a deep and meaningful acreage of single-sex ground.

I am clearing up the aftermath of a Lego explosion one evening when I receive a text from Kindred MOB.

'Turn on TV, now. US!'

Intrigued, I do as I am told. A documentary, it seems, where parents of only girls swap places for a weekend with those of an all-boy brood. Now this, I think, grinning to myself, I'd like to see.

Surprisingly, given the Western world's current preoccupation with entirely unrealistic reality TV, both families are refreshingly normal. Yes, the female family's life revolves around nail varnish and Next, and yes, the boy zone is dominated by rugby and railways, but not in an off-the-edge, overly extreme kind of way.

For while indoors, the picture-perfect girls immerse both themselves and their shell-shocked bedroom floors in paraphernalia – mostly plastic, mainly pink – outside, they indulge in sport and play long and loud.

The boys meanwhile, although wild proponents of madness and mud, are also taught how to clear up, how to cook, how to care. Like me, the featured multiple MOB is happy to be caterer, cleaner and plasterer of cuts. But also, like me, she refuses to be viewed as a domestic doormat.

Whatever the gender, suggests the show, whether the kids' floors are covered in palaces or pirates, parenting has both its messy and its downright marvellous moments.

So far – so girl, so boy – so good.

But the part that really rings bells – the part which I recount in detail to the FOB later that night on the phone – is when the 'outnumbered' parent (the mother of boys or the father of girls) becomes aware of their own repressed expectations of life.

'The glitter-girl dad,' I explain excitedly, 'the one who spends most of his weekends in mascara and Monsoon, takes his "borrowed boys" to the race track. It makes him remember the thrill of speed, reawakens his love of sport . . . something he has "buried" since becoming a multiple FOG. By being with boys he seems to kind of . . . rediscover . . . the competitive edge to his oestrogen-overwhelmed self.'

I pause for breath, while the FOB (I'd like to think) pauses for thought.

'The "he–she MOB" meanwhile, the one who is more at home hollering at mud-encrusted males than in Costa coffee, follows the lead of her deputising daughters, and rediscovers her long-forgotten love of horse-riding. For once, she does some-thing that *she* really wants to do, rather than automatically participating in the pursuits of her boy-heavy household.'

Summary over, I await his response. Silence.

Then: 'So you want to start riding again? Do you want to get a horse?' he asks hesitantly, in his fact-following fashion.

'No, of course I don't want to get a horse. Where on earth would we put it?' I retort. 'And anyway, I'm way too wobbly to be wearing jodhpurs! No, the point is that being the odd one out, as the only XX in a household of XYs, it can feel, just occasionally, as if I'm following the flow of the male majority, rather than . . . than . . . maybe carving my own, more feminine, channel!'

I hope that this suitably manly analogy will help him understand my obviously over-emotional female vent.

'You mean you want to do your own damming next time we're at the beach, instead of just watching us do ours?' he asks hopefully. 'That would be great. I always thought you preferred reading your book . . . liked a bit of peace and quiet. But if that's not the case, then great, *great*! Definitely: all hands to the pump – the more, the merrier!'

I haven't the heart to inform my endearingly enthusiastic FOB that I have not, after all, developed an overwhelming penchant for what is, as far as I am still concerned, the utterly pointless redistribution of rocks. Instead, I sigh, scoop a stray blue brick from under the sofa with my pink slipper and admit defeat. It's probably just easier, I think, and certainly simpler, to quietly subsume my female self for the greater good of my males. I turn off the TV and head for bed and my book.

Thus, thanks to experience, Grant and eye-opening documentaries, I begin to welcome the inevitable realities of being a MOB.

Beginning with football, and finishing goodness knows where, I decide to give up fighting the testosterone tide. 'Cos if I can't beat 'em,' acknowledges this 'sex specialist in the making', 'then I might as well join 'em!'

And join 'em I do.

So when Feisty Fellow presents me with a blank sheet of paper four sodden days into the spring half term, I resist the temptation to delegate to Dad. Instead, I rise to the challenge and set about mastering the most male of skill sets. I learn how to make a paper plane.

With unanticipated enthusiasm, I concentrate on the creases, nip sharp the wings, tweak the nose into place for a turbulence-free take-off. Astoundingly simple, yet astonishingly satisfying. No matter that within seconds my plane nose-dives into the washing-up water, and I spend the next half an hour placating my now verging-on-the-hysterical smallest son. No matter that my twin prop will never look like a turbo. No matter. I am embarking on a journey, I tell myself proudly, towards specialising in *my* sex.

Then, when, five domestic days into the Easter holidays, my males head outside to build yet another boys' bonfire, I abandon the cooking and scurry to their side.

'But you don't like bonfires, Mum! You always say they're a waste of time . . . that they just smoke out the washing!' they comment bemused, as I haul holly and ash on to the flaming pile.

'Oh yeah?' I retort, red-faced with exertion and exhilaration as my cunningly lain logs go pleasingly up in smoke. 'Can I borrow your poker?' I say, grabbing an astonished Binary Boy's stick to resurrect the rapidly diminishing flames.

'You're actually quite good at this, Mum!' comments Sensible Son.

Racing now down *my* sex-specialising highway, I bluster and beam with maternal MOB pride.

And when, after seventeen deceptively sunny days of making sand sandwiches, I decide I've finally had enough of being picnic-provider-in-chief, I squeeze my body into a full-length wetsuit and join my boys in their aquatic adventures. We frolic like dolphins in the glacial West Country waters, until hunger pangs penetrate even the numbest of minds.

As I haul myself back on to the beach – more whale than dolphin without the benefit of buoyancy – my ever-ready beloved races on ahead.

'I've got to capture this moment for posterity!' he exclaims, brandishing the camera.

'Oh no you don't!' I shriek, visions of my wetsuit-clad carcass on our Facebook page flashing unappetisingly in front of my eyes. 'Either the camera goes or now is the first and last time you'll ever see me in this!'

The wetsuit – and its wrinkled, but warm, now fully fledged 'sexpert' – live to savour another sea.

From dame-in-denial to completely conversant MOB in three straightforward, but highly significant, strides.

The great thing, however, about any journey that involves trying to change a woman's mindset, is to appreciate when the destination has been reached and thus it's safer to stop.

Unfortunately for the men in this honorary-man-mum's life, they push my new-found 'join 'em' philosophy one tank too far.

It's one of those days when you can't quite believe it's still August and you contemplate – semi-seriously this time – moving, permanently, to warmer climes. Outside, the rain hammers down, drowning the Crocs and caps that lie discarded on the lawn, already distant memories of the briefest sojourn of sunshine that was, apparently, our summer.

Inside, boy bedlam.

In the absence of exercise and with screens switched off, the boys embark on another of their favourite pastimes: den building.

Outside, in the open air and with the help of the odd tree or two, I can see the attraction of den building. In the sitting room, with no air and involving all available furniture, cushions and cuddly toys, I'm afraid I cannot.

If the camp was camped in, I wouldn't mind. But that, apparently, is not the point. The moment sofas have been shifted, pillows piled and teddies trampled, the game is over. Fun finished. The camp, once built, lies deserted and dark. The sofa, however, free from padding, becomes instead a temporary trampoline, a homemade soft-play area, a recipe for disaster.

Sensible Son executes a perfect forward roll, narrowly missing my favourite picture with his overly long limbs. I've had enough.

'Right,' I scream, trying desperately to compete with my kangaroo kids. 'Right, put your shoes on, boys – we're going out!'

Train track scatters as Feisty Fellow sneaks in one last leap. Sensing that even his recently reformed 'male' mum may not appreciate this demonstration of his Superman skills, he scuttles, for once, obediently to the door.

'Totally Tank' announces the craftily camouflaged sign. Below the sign is, unsurprisingly, a tank.

'Wow/cool/awesome!' shriek the children from the back rows of the second-hand Citroën which has now replaced our redundant Scenic. Seven seats, nearly two metres tall. Avoiding underground car parks seems a small price to pay for banishing boy bickering.

The FOB turns to me and smiles happily, cat got the cream. 'I told you they'd love this!' he grins. 'Cor, look at the tracks on that!'

Stifling what has become an almost overwhelming urge to drive straight past the entrance and on to, well, frankly *anywhere* else, I manoeuvre my own tank into the car park. A car park that is filled with row upon row of what look suspiciously like fellow MOB-mobiles: battered buses full of surfboards and sand. Not a 'Babe on Board' sticker in sight.

We pull up next to a carbon-copy car complete with carbon-copy kids.

Catching the eye of the fellow MOB, I smile sympathetically. Her face bears a lamb-to-the-slaughter look as she follows her excited flock towards the entrance. I run through the puddles to catch up with my own stampeding herd.

Inside, I am transported swiftly back to the seven-year-old me who went to the fair and ended up being dragged into a tantalising, but terrifying, House of Horrors. Round and round I went, down this passageway and that, desperate to find the elusive exit. Witches and wizards on every corner, evil eyes following my every move.

Only here, the eyes are replaced by stuffed soldiers, the creepy creatures by . . . tanks.

Attempting enthusiasm befitting of the 'sexpert' I am, I stop to read the first sign by the first tank. I peruse the second. I skim read the third. By tank number twenty-six, I have lost both the boys and – increasingly – the will to live. Lured forward by the whiff of fresh coffee, I guiltily skirt the 'Birth of the Tank' section (the memories of Feisty Fellow's watery arrival into this world still fractionally too painful) and head for the café.

As, it appears, has virtually every other MOB from the car park. Table upon table laden with ladies, visibly shell-shocked and nursing their coffees like the elixir of life. Row upon row of women with expressions more often sported by their husbands, plonked outside the ladies' changing rooms during an M&S sale.

Sensing solidarity in numbers, I join the queue.

Halfway through my drink, I am joined by my males. Breathless and flushed, they rush up to the table.

'Isn't it cool, Mum?' they screech. 'Did you see that M1 Abrams . . . it's got a top speed of *forty-five mph* and more horsepower than a Lamborghini! Now that's what I call awesome!'

The FOB flashes me a grin, eyes sparkling. 'Mind if we head back to the exhibition area for a minute or two? There's a special bit about the Birth of the Tank that the boys – well, all of us actually – really want to see. You coming?'

'I've . . . er . . . I've already done that bit, thanks. But you head off. I'm fine here. I'll just finish my coffee and then catch you up.'

Three cups of caffeine later, I can put it off no longer. Bladder bursting and head spinning, I trudge resignedly back to the trenches, joining the unenthusiastic throng of female foot soldiers heading for the front line.

'Well, wasn't that a success?' glows the FOB as we make our way – finally – out of the door and into the suddenly appetising rain.

I glare at the back of his head, eyes aching, head pounding, feet killing.

'Hey, look!' he cries, stopping to read the notice by the exit. 'It says here that we can come back as many times as we like for a whole year after one visit . . . for free! Shall we sign up?'

He turns, smiling, but even he cannot fail to read my black and white MOB message.

'Errr – just a thought . . . no, maybe not. Once is probably enough. Best to quit while you're still ahead.'

His after all *fundamentally female* 'sexpert' nods – 'Absolutely' – and we jog away from 'Totally Tank', to board the MOB-mobile, in the rain.

Ten things you enjoy doing as a MOB that you didn't think you would

- Putting together an Airfix model. OK, so it's broken within seconds – but that's not the point.
- Discovering the Horrors of Henry.
- Rediscovering the joys of chess.
- Forgetting the 'joys' of pottering around town.
- Wearing a wetsuit. So, it doesn't look great, but, hey, it's preferable to pneumonia.
- Geomag.
- Collecting pocketfuls of gun cartridges on a wintery walk and taking them dutifully back home, instead of following your instincts and throwing them in the bin.
- Marble runs.
- Football . . . even if Mum's *always* in goal.
- Watching an ever-deeper pile of ever-more-huge shoes. And loving each and every smelly son-scuffed one.

And the five things that you just will not now, or ever, do . . .

- Show boys how to clean their bits in the bath . . . that is something that should always be delegated to Dad.
- Discuss in detail the evolvement and HP of each and every bloomin' Pokemon.
- Spend an entire weekend watching sport (any, including football) on TV. Live: possibly; on a screen: in *his* dreams.
- Participate in ice-smashing sorties on the way to school, obviously wearing as little season-appropriate clothing as possible.
- Museums involving vehicles of any shape or form. Fully fledged MOB maybe – but don't push it.

LESSON 12:

Always call a son a spade

My boys have inherited much from the FOB.

All three have great appetites, all three have good teeth and all three can disarm almost anyone with a mischievous grin. Less fortunately, they also appear to have been blessed with his uncanny ability to put his size 12s firmly in it. The difference is that while the FOB restricts his inadvertent displays of tactlessness to me and – generally – my hair, our boys have yet to grasp the more subtle, but vital, aspects of emotional intelligence.

As, one sunny day in early October, I am about to find out.

It's breakfast time in the Evans household. Three heads, varying shades of blondy-brown, bend over their bowls, downing syrupy porridge at a ridiculous rate. Goldilocks wouldn't even get a look in here, I'm afraid.

'Slow down, folks . . . please!' I beg. 'There's no rush!'

The heads stay down. I am obviously talking to the boy brick wall. I try again.

'Hey. Sensible Son . . . Binary Boy . . . Feisty Fellow,' – I vaguely remember reading that you have to address boys directly, by name, to stand any chance of them hearing, let alone understanding, what you're saying – 'take it easy with the porridge, will you!'

Two heads stay put. Only Sensible Son looks up for a second.

'Pardon, Mum?' he asks politely. I sigh, incredulously. How can he be sitting two feet away from me and not hear what I'm saying? Still, at least I've got *his* attention.

'I said,' I repeat, raising my voice just a fraction, 'slow . . . it . . . down. There's no hurry!'

'But there is, Mum,' he says, glancing at the clock. 'Gotta get to school early today. Swimming, remember?'

'Oh yes,' I groan. While *I* had forgotten, *he* obviously hadn't. 'Why did you leave it till *now* to remind me? Oh, never mind . . . run upstairs and find your kit.'

Five minutes later, he's still not down.

'I can't find it!' he yells from the depths of his room.

'Have you looked?' I yell back.

'Yeasss . . . where is it?'

'In your cupboard,' I shout, before adding in a learned-from-substantial-experience-of-men-looking-for-things fashion, 'third shelf down, on the right, at the front, in the bright yellow bag.'

'Oh right . . .' Silence. Then, 'Nope, still can't see it – 'snot there.'

I fling down the drying-up towel and stomp upstairs. Reach into his cupboard, third shelf down, on the right, at the front, and brandish a bright yellow bag in front of his face.

'Oh, *that* yellow bag . . .' he says, spit-image and spit-sound of his 'man look' dad. We clatter back to the kitchen to rejoin his brothers at the table.

'My teacher's 'avin' a baby!' announces Feisty Fellow, mid-mouthful.

'Is she? How do you know?' quizzes Binary Boy, amazed that such an important piece of information has escaped his inquisitive, but at times selectively deaf, ears.

'Told us,' says his smaller brother smugly. 'But she only told our class . . . tomorrow.'

'Yesterday . . . you mean she told you yesterday, not tomorrow!' corrects Binary Boy.

'Oh yeah, sorry. Yesterday,' laughs a mid-porridge happy Feisty Fellow. 'Maybe she'll tell the rest of the school errlee'r.'

'Earlier? You mean later, *silly!*' corrects his sibling again.

I look fearfully at Feisty Fellow; wait for the outraged explosion. But it doesn't happen. Hmm, I think gratefully, maybe that Testosterone Fairy was busy elsewhere last night.

'That's very exciting, isn't it?' I say to my youngest son. 'She'll be able to tell you all about her pregnancy . . . the baby. You'll be able to watch as her baby bump grows bigger and bigger.'

Feisty Fellow nods enthusiastically, mouth too full of food to comment further. He swallows, looks up at me, declares: 'You look like you're having a baby too, Mummy . . . you've got a fat tummy!'

My turn to swallow and look down at what I had hoped was a fairly flat(ish) stomach. Not *that* bad for the amount of toing and froing it's had to endure over the years, anyway. Apparently though, not that good either.

Binary Boy pipes up to defend his deflated mum. 'She hasn't got a big tummy!' he retaliates.

'Oh yes she has,' countermands my youngest, pointing towards my now sucked-in stomach, '*and* she's got boobies!'

Binary Boy pipes up again. 'But she *is* a girl and *all* girls have boobies, don't they, Mum? As soon as they're fifteen.'

Where on earth is this conversation heading, I wonder? This time it's me looking worriedly at my watch, and not just my eldest son. I'm not sure I've got either the time or the inclination to embark on the birds-and-bees blurb with ten minutes to go before we set off for school.

'Hmm, kind of . . .' I say, and then, ever mindful of my role as sole provider of sex-balanced body image, I add, 'although it might not always be obvious; some girls will have larger breasts, others' will be smaller, won't they? Everyone's different.'

Middle son nods wisely. His younger brother has already lost interest and abandoned the table. Sensible Son, characteristically silent as he chews over both his porridge and the conversation, has, as ever, the last word. 'Yeah, and some are truly *teeny* like yours, aren't they, Mum?'

'Gee thanks!' I say, despondently, putting down – and throwing in – the drying-up towel.

'But it's true, Mum, isn't it?' he frowns, blatantly unaware that there could ever be a more emotionally acceptable alternative to speaking the truth, the whole truth . . . and nothing but.

True it may be, I think, but you don't need to be quite so straightforward . . . so blunt . . . so *male* about it, do you? Even if it *is* a spade, you don't always need to call it one. Maybe you could try calling it a more complimentary trowel instead, or even a fork? I force a smile at my literal son's inadvertent insult.

So, big stomach, small boobs – and all before half-eight in the morning. 'Is that all folks?' I ask. They nod happily, put on their coats and set off for school.

But it's not quite all, no. There is, apparently, plenty more where that came from.

The next day, I'm approached at school by Feisty Fellow's teacher.

'Mrs Evans,' she says, 'I wanted to catch you!'

My stomach plummets. However kind, however gentle, a tap on the shoulder by a Miss or Sir can reduce even the most assertive of adults to schoolgirl jelly.

'Everything OK with Feisty Fellow? I hope he's been behaving himself?' I chuckle nervously. 'Oh, and by the way, I hear congratulations are in order!'

'Yes, thanks,' she replies, glowing and smoothing the planes of her still-flat stomach. Her train of thought, however, won't be derailed. 'I just wanted a quick word.'

There's a gurgling pit in the bottom of my belly, and I begin to glow ever so slightly myself. Or possibly 'perspire', maybe even 'sweat'.

'Don't worry. It's nothing too serious.' My heart rate calms a fraction, returning from the danger zone to somewhere just above normal. 'We were talking about my pregnancy this morning, about when the baby would be born, and your son . . .'

Oh God. He hasn't been describing the mating habits of a Hampshire Hog, has he? Or gone on about the Aberdeen Angus eating its own afterbirth? Please tell me he hasn't drawn a picture of the extra-large attributes of the newly acquired ram? I just knew there would be unfortunate repercussions of spending the holiday with Good-life Gran, getting a live – and possibly deadly – introduction to sex.

With an impending sense of doom, I wait to find out what pearls of learned wisdom my youngest has been scattering over his schoolboy chums.

'He was very excited about it all . . . said he couldn't wait. What for, I asked him – and do you know what the answer was?' She is, I sense, while mostly amused, just a modicum put out. 'Not for the bump or the baby. No, what he couldn't wait for, was to watch me get . . . FAT!'

I let out a burst of bated breath. Is that all? Thank goodness, I think. It could have been *so* much worse!

'I'm so sorry,' I babble, deeply relieved, 'but I think that might have been my fault. We were talking about it this morning . . .' I decide to quit while I'm ahead. 'I think he may have got his mind in a bit of a muddle!' I say, making a dash for the door.

'Hmm,' she says, schoolmarm smoothly. 'A muddle indeed.'

★ ★ ★

Later that evening, the boys are squished in the bath. For once, they sit quietly, ducks in a row, focused on making bubbles in plastic pots. I make the most of the uncustomary calm.

'What *are* you doing, Mum?' asks Sensible Son, craning his head over the side of the tub.

'I'm doing . . . my . . . exercises!' I puff, as I hoist my shoulders painfully from the floor. I am trying (in vain) to remember what the Body Beautiful aerobics teacher had said about imagining an orange – or maybe it was a melon? – between your chest and your chin as you attempt to sit up.

'But *why* are you doing exercises?' asks Binary Boy. 'What's the point?'

Judging by this morning's flabby feedback, I think glumly, very little. Still, it's worth a try.

'To work my stomach muscles – keep them strong, so that my tummy isn't all floppy and loose.' Proud possessors of bouncy-boy six-packs, they stare at me, unconvinced. So I explain further. 'When you've had a baby, your muscles are stretched, aren't they, as your tummy gets bigger. So you have to work hard afterwards, if you want to get them back!'

Sensible Son strokes his soapy scientific beard with contemplative fingers. 'But you had Feisty Fellow years and years ago. Surely they should be back to normal by *now*!'

'Well, yes,' I harrumph, legs in the air. 'They . . . probably . . . should. But just like you,' I point out, 'they don't *always* do as they're told.'

'Well . . .' he reflects again, demonstrating his own advanced aptitude for convenient hearing, 'I really would have thought they should be back to normal by *now*.'

Conversation apparently over, he goes, somewhat incongruously, back to his bubbles.

★ ★ ★

As ever, it's my female friends who come to my mental rescue.

Kindred MOB and I are gathered together at the home of our brave friend Perfect Pair for our monthly moan. Seven sons and one Gorgeous (but, luckily, hold-her-own) Girl are cavorting around the house, playing a mixture of drums, pianos and air guitars. Subtly and sensibly, Perfect Pair shuts the kitchen door and we huddle round the hob for safety and chat.

A maternal therapy session, we share our children's latest cringe-worthy crimes. Amid understanding hilarity, I recount Feisty Fellow's most recent 'fat faux pas'.

'It wasn't *really* his fault,' I try to convince myself, as much as my friends. 'He just doesn't seem to have grasped what is, and more importantly isn't, acceptable to say in public yet. He didn't mean to cause offence; he was just saying it as he thought it was!'

Kindred MOB grins. 'I once spent most of a very embarrassing train journey trying to tell the boys – quietly – to stop staring and pointing at a particularly unusual-looking lady with a virtually bald head and monster make-up. "But she *has* got no hair, her eyes *are* bright white and she *does* look like a Death Eater!" they kept protesting loudly when I told them to pipe down. They just didn't get it!'

We smile. Perfect Pair adds her balanced view to our all-boy debate.

'The thing is, I think boys generally *are* more straight-talking than girls. Just like their dads, really. They look, they ask, they say what they see. They're not particularly bothered about the underlying whys and wherefores – about how what they're saying might make you feel, about whether it's always appropriate or not. Tactless maybe, but perhaps more honest as a result. My boy's certainly more straightforward than his sister!'

She stops as her son bursts into the kitchen and runs to her side, tears coursing down his sweaty face.

'*He* hit me with a drumstick,' he sobs, 'on purpose. And it *really* hurts . . . here!'

She cuddles him close – 'Oooh, my poor munchkin'; kisses the proffered body part – 'I think you'll live!'; pushes him gently towards the door – 'Off you go and play!'

Obediently, her son wipes the snot from his nose with his sleeve, gives her a wobbly grin and rushes back to his already-forgotten foe. 'Coming . . . ready or not!' he yells, swallowing a sob and racing up the stairs.

MOBs and MOG watch his astonishing, yet unsurprisingly quick, recovery with knowing smiles.

Then, using the specialised skill set developed over years of maternal *conversationus interruptus*, we resume our discussion at the precise point we left off. Perfect Pair picks up the thread.

'It's the same with relationships . . . with friends. Boys generally aren't overly complicated: they're either happy or they're sad. And if they're sad, it doesn't normally take too long to get to the bottom of it and sort it out. Either that or they give the problem a short, sharp shove and move on. Now if that,' she gestures towards the door through which her son has just disappeared, 'if that had been an incident involving his little sister, it would've been a much more convoluted kettle of female fish!'

I reflect on what she's said. Think of all the times my boys have slammed the door on me one minute, snuggled in the next. When in the in-breath they hate him, on the out- are best friends. When after breakfast I'm the 'worst mother', after lunch I'm 'the best'. Confrontation in our house is often vocal, sometimes violent, but at least it's short-lived.

'Girls are totally different,' continues Perfect Pair. 'They may be more empathetic at times, but they're also more complex – trickier to understand. Remember yourself as a teenager? The anxieties, the insecurities, the best-friend shenanigans? It starts amazingly early – even six-year-olds seem to twist what's being said, constantly fall in and out with their friends . . . It's rarely black and white in a mini-woman's world; more of a . . . a kind of deep, murky rainbow of intense emotion!' She finishes with a flourish, hands flapping wildly like an irate Italian.

Even us potentially boy-battered, boy-blinded MOBs can sense that this is coming from her Perfect Pair heart.

'Phew!' says Kindred MOB. 'Suddenly having to replaster and paint the hallway every six months doesn't seem quite so bad compared to understanding the whys and wherefores of the junior female brain!'

There appears to be some truth, then, in what some clever person (hopefully, a suitably qualified Perfect Pair parent) once said. Boys may mess with your house, but girls are much better at messing with your mind. And while walls can be wiped and mud can be mopped, an oestrogen outburst is substantially more complex to clean.

Perfect Pair nods vigorously. 'Absolutely! Boys may be harder physical work when they're little, but at least when they're older they just grunt and go to ground. God help me when my daughter hits puberty and the pub – she'll be enough to drive anyone, including me, to drink!'

'Ah . . . the "p" word!' says Kindred MOB, turning slightly pale and skipping deftly on to the next therapy topic. Another example of the maternal skill set. 'Have you had the birds-and-bees chat yet?'

Perfect Pair shakes her head, thankfully.

'Not really,' I admit. 'I'm kind of hoping to leave it to the cockerels and the cows . . .'

Kindred MOB lets this random comment pass – she's met Good-life Gran – and groans. 'Me neither,' she says, 'but at the rate they're growing up, it won't be long!'

How right you are, as ever, Kindred MOB. For conversations XX and discussions Y are right around the chromosomal corner.

We're back at Good-life Gran's for another half-term break.

On day one of the holiday, their Felicity Kendal GOB teaches the boys how to trim sheep's feet without drawing blood from either their own, or the unfortunate ewe's, extremities.

On day two, she shows them how to insert sausage meat into its silky-smooth skin, having, of course, first killed and then cut up the ill-fated porker.

On day three, their Farmer Nan lets them loose with mud, sand and straw as they relearn and revel in the art of cladding both themselves and an incidental pigsty with a liberal coating of globby cob clay.

With the boys, quite literally, like pigs in mud, I'm beginning to wonder how even my manic mother can keep up this momentum till the end of the week.

What I don't know, however, is that she has the AI experience up her boiler-suited sleeve.

Eight forty-six a.m., day four. The boys are already outside a'feeding the flocks.

I, meanwhile, am buried in my bed under a particularly decadent duvet, when I am rudely awoken by smallest son. Still half-asleep, I don't automatically welcome him with the most open of arms.

'What-ish-it?' I slur, forcing one reluctant eye open in response to his unexpected rousing.

'You've gotta call the AA – now!' he pants. I open the other eye to better examine my emphatic child. Head to toe in mud-encrusted waterproofs and wellies, he appears to be steaming like a muck heap on an autumn morning. And, I think, as I'm assaulted by his aroma, he most certainly smells like one.

'The AA?' I say, rubbing my eyes and holding my nose. 'At this time in the morning? Why?'

'Bluebell's jumping on Buttercup. Good-life Gran says you have to call the AA man straight away. Quick, Mum,' he hollers, grabbing the duvet with his brown paws, 'it's 'portant!'

'Oh, *that* kind of AA man!' I grasp, sleep-slow.

Sensing that I am not about to get away with turning the other cheek on this one, I wipe his hand off the bedclothes and head for the phone.

Forty minutes later, we're mid-full-fry when a van draws up.

'The AA's here!' shouts Feisty Fellow, leaping from the table and pulling on his boots. His elder brothers down forks to follow his mud-splattered trail. What on earth are they expecting to see, I wonder, fearing that they may well be disappointed by the absence of a tow truck and flashing lights. Somewhat reluctantly, I put my own breakfast in the oven and step outside.

By the time I reach the barn where the AI man is to do the deed, the boys are perched – spellbound – on the five-bar gate. The amorous cow is caught in the cattle crush innocently munching nuts, while the Artificial Inseminator examines, with interest, her resplendent rear end.

Man on the moon in his protective green garb, Mr AI fishes into his bag and pulls out a pair of long latex gloves. Expertly, he snaps them on, covering his hands, his wrists and, slightly worryingly, the remainder of his arms right up to, and actually over, his elbows. He reaches into his bag again and pulls out a lethal-looking syringe. Tapping the tip of the needle ominously with the back of his nail, he squirts a sample drop or two of 'bull' out of the top.

Instinctively, I clamp my legs together and cringe. 'Poor cow!' I murmur, more than happy – for once – to be human.

'What did you say, Mummy?' asks Feisty Fellow, turning his

head towards me. There is obviously nothing wrong with his ears today.

'Nothing!' I reply hurriedly.

The boys continue to watch from the gate – open-mouthed – awaiting the AI man's next masterly move. They are not disappointed.

With one deft dive, he thrusts his begloved arm right up the backside of the oblivious bovine, while with the other he inserts his needle into the appropriate hole. As he plunges the syringe home, the cow takes the opportunity to empty her bowels on to both the straw and, in the process, his offending arm.

This is too much for even my countryside kids.

'Arghh . . . that sucks . . .' screams Sensible Son. 'Truly gross!'

'Did you see that, Mum? Mum, did you see what Bluebell did!' screeches Binary Boy.

'Euurgh . . . what did he do that for?' shrieks Feisty Fellow. 'Why'd he put his hand up *there*? How on urf does *that* help Bluebell have a *baby*?'

I look round in desperation for Good-life Gran, hoping she can help explain the strange-but-true facts of livestock life. Unfortunately for me, she is otherwise engaged.

'Er . . . he . . . um . . . well . . .' Then, like the syringe, I take the plunge. 'Well,' I embark slowly, giving myself time to think, 'if there's not a daddy cow – a bull – around, then the AI man needs to help. He brings some . . . er . . . some of the bull's . . . um . . . seed here with him and then . . . errr . . . just like you saw, he puts it . . . into the cow. Then, hopefully, in a few months' time, Bluebell will have a calf.'

I look at him, praying that my embarrassingly abbreviated lesson in the sex life of a Devon Red will temporarily satisfy his five-year-old brain. Feisty Fellow nods thoughtfully. It appears to have done the trick.

'Don't think I wanna be a AA man when I'm olda any more!' he declares, eyeing the still-steaming straw with obvious disgust. 'Can I go and have my bacon 'n' eggs now, Mummy?'

Somehow, I don't think *I'll* be finishing my full-fry any time soon.

The following week, we are back at school. Back to black shoes instead of wet wellies, back to the curriculum instead of country life. And I'm back to the washing machine, no lie-ins and work.

Over an after-school supper, we chew the daily cud.

Amid phonemes and phonics, I tell the part-time FOB about a TV programme I'd watched in his absence the previous night.

'It was about "Octomom" – you know, the American lady who has octuplets and who already had six kids; fourteen under ten under one roof. Can you imagine? And they say our house can be chaotic!'

'Are the children boys or girls?' asks our increasingly gender-conscious eldest son.

'Both, I think . . . Anyway, I'm not sure when you get to those numbers it really makes much difference! And,' I add, 'she's a single mum . . . no dad around to help.'

'What? She puts out her own bins?' says Binary Boy, ridiculously incredulous.

'*And* checks her own tyre pressures . . .' adds Sensible Son, knowledgably.

'What? Her kids don't even get no banoffee pie, like what Dad makes every time you go away for the night?' despairs Feisty Fellow.

I smile and shake my head. Their sexual stereotypes, like their lack of tact, obviously still need some significant work. Their eyes, however, mist over: they're totally sharing her pie-free pain. When it comes to food – if not to people – their capacity for empathy is undoubtedly alive.

Feisty Fellow cocks his head to one side, chews on his tongue. His mind's still lamenting the loss of the pie.

Apparently not.

'But if there's no dad, how did she get all them babies?' He blinks, squints; he's thinking hard. '*You* said at Good-life Gran's that you need a boy cow to help a mummy cow make a calf . . .' He hesitates again, putting my partially explained X and Y together and getting . . . confused. 'So – did the AA man come along wif his gloves and his van, and stick some "bull" up that 'Merican lady's butt too?'

The FOB is aghast.

His brothers are amused. As much by his Simpsonesque 'butt', as his impeccable, but misplaced, lady-led logic.

'Don't be daft, Feisty Fellow. That's not right!' admonishes Binary Boy.

Phew, I think, maybe my 'cop-out' explanation of the procreation process *had* been clear enough, after all. Maybe I had been sufficiently straight-talking for my mini-men to grasp the fundamental, if not the full, facts of life.

But Binary Boy continues: 'It's not Mr *AA* who would stuff his hand up her butt to get her pregnant, silly. Mr AA's the mechanic who changes Mum's tyres when we break down by the road.' The FOB looks at me – news to him; I shrug and smile. 'No . . . it would be Mr *AI*!'

The time has come, then. Conversation chromosomes, solar-system sex. This definitely calls for a man-to-man – and not male-to-MOB – moment.

'Over to you!' I delegate hastily to my still-speechless spouse, 'I'm off to aerobics to work on my flab!'

Top ten phrases known to MOB

- Get down!
- Be careful/gentle!; I said, BE CAREFUL/GENTLE!
- Did you hear me?
- Oooh, you're *so* like your father!
- Will you put your shoes on? Have you put your shoes on yet? PUT YOUR SHOES ON NOW!
- Just because . . . that's why.
- Can you STOP picking/licking/flicking (all of the above and simultaneously) . . . please.
- Just SIT STILL.
- No, not there. I said *in* the loo . . .
- Aw, please . . . can you put it away . . .

A Lady-led approach to the Fundamental Facts of Life

Do not:

- Tell your tot that the Tampax in your handbag is Mummy's special sweet . . . unless, of course, you accept that he'll take the inevitable next step.
- Tell your boy that he didn't actually come out of the place where you wee . . . unless, of course, you're willing to put the evidence on show.
- Tell your son that the roadkill on the lane is just having a kip . . . unless, of course, you're happy that he brings it back home and puts it to bed.
- Tell your child that calling someone 'sexy' is like saying they're pretty . . . unless, of course, you're comfortable with him telling his teacher she's looking super-sexy today.
- Tell your male that he consists mostly of little fish and an egg . . . unless, of course, you're an expert at cooking vegan cuisine.

What the MOB says . . .	And what the boy hears . . .
'Go upstairs and get dressed!'	'Zoom to my room, fling PJs on the floor, pull on some pants . . . and then crouch on the carpet and play with my Lego.'
'Slow down!'	'Carry on, carry on – preferably faster and more furiously than before.'
'Will you sit on your bottom, please!'	'Sit on my knees? Sure! Or a mountain of cushions/two chair legs/my brother. I'm up for anything . . . but please, not my behind.'
'Wash your hands before we eat.'	'Meander in the direction of the bathroom, maybe even enter. Wave hands under just about dripping cold tap (no soap, obviously – soap is for girls), dry paws on filthy shirt and sit down for supper.'
'No toys at the table.'	'Well, obviously she can't mean me . . . and anyway my DS is not, strictly speaking, a toy.'
'Get off that computer – NOW!'	'Yup . . . nearly there . . . just finishing this level/match/game . . . yes . . . just coming . . . in a minute (or sixty).'
'Shhh, I'm on the phone.'	'Shout anything inappropriate at the top of my voice. "I need a POOOO!" is always a good one.'
'Let's go . . . I said, "Let's go!" . . . Did you hear, me? LET'S GO! . . . Oh, never mind, I'll go by myself.'	'Dad . . . where's Mum?'

Fairies is for *gerls*, bicarb is for boys

It would be safe to say that I've had more than my fair share of men in my life.

From my dad to Big Brother to my best-friend FOB, from my number-one son, number-two and then three, I have, by anyone's standards, had both the motive and the means to learn much about living with the opposite sex.

And it is true that I have learned that I am *naturally* more comfortable bathed in blue, rather than trying – in defiance of my MOB status and, actually, *myself* – to look pretty in pink. And it is also true that I have learned to accept, and even embrace, the – initially instinctively fem-alien – realities of my boy-heavy world.

You might be forgiven, therefore, for thinking that by now I would also totally understand what goes on – not only on the outside – but also *inside* my boys' heads. That I would be completely au fait with the mindset of the male.

If that *is* what you're thinking, if you're giving me clairvoyant credit, then you'd be wrong. Because despite the tons of theory and the aeons of experience, I nevertheless find myself – frequently – baffled and bewildered by what really makes my boys *tick*. And a baking bonanza is just one case in point.

'Let's make fairy cakes!' I suggest one Saturday afternoon, gazing dismally out of the window at the bucketing rain. Even if we haven't been out yet today and the pups are beginning to play 'It' up the stairs, and even if we have got good waterproofs and wellies, even *I* am not going out in *that*.

'Fairy cakes? Fairies is for *gerls*!' says the advert-indoctrinated Feisty Fellow. CBeebies is now CBabies and they've discovered ITV.

'Yeah . . . for girls! They're pink and sparkly . . . and . . . like totally yeuck!' middle son joins in with vehemence and venom.

'Don't be so ridiculous,' I say, reaching for my marge-mouldy recipe book. 'There's nothing "girly" about fairy cakes . . . it's just what they're called, that's all. They taste exactly the same as any other type of cake. Come on, let's make some. And if you're really good, you can lick out the bowl when we've finished!' They prick up their ears at the prospect of food. 'Anyway,' I post-script, 'you don't seem to mind the tooth *fairy* bringing you money when you lose a tooth, do you?'

'That's different,' says Binary Boy, butting his bottom lip.

'Hmm,' I say, turning back to Nigella.

'OK, OK,' he backs down. 'But if we're making fairy cakes,' – I pull up his stool – 'can we make the icing blue?'

(Overtly) boy blue icing on (apparently) female fairy cakes . . . well, that obviously makes all the difference! Now why didn't *I* think of that?

'Right, what do we need?' I mutter, head in the cupboard. 'Flour . . . sugar . . . baking powder . . . bicarb – bicarb. Where is my bicarb? I had nearly a whole pot in here the other day, I'm sure I did. Where's it gone?'

Binary Boy looks slightly concerned. 'Is bicarb the same as bicarbonate of soda? In a white container? I . . . er . . . I think I might have . . . umm . . . finished it.'

'Finished it? How can you finish an entire pot of bicarbonate of soda? Oh God, you didn't think it was sugar and eat it, did you?' I look at him anxiously for signs of bicarb-induced rabies – a frothing at the mouth, perhaps? Unusual swellings?

Thankfully, he appears to be totally normal.

'I . . . er . . . it wasn't my fault, Mum. It wasn't!' he shrieks clocking my less-than-understanding look. 'It was Sensible Son's . . . He told me to get it . . . for the experiment – to make a volcano. He said they did it at school – that it was awesome!'

Volcano? 'So where is this . . . this "volcano" now?' I ask. I may switch off to the boys' more bizarre behaviour at times, but surely even I would have noticed a volcano in our midst?

He gestures towards the bin. 'In there. We put it in there once it'd stopped erupting. You should've seen it, Mum. It was worth using the whole pot. It went *every*where . . . all over the table . . . the floor!' His eyes fizz with delight at the memory of his lava fountain.

The volcano is not the only thing to erupt. 'The floor?! What do you mean it went on the floor?'

'Oh, not *too* much,' he says hastily, 'and we managed to get it all up. At least, I think we did. Did stink a bit of vinegar though!'

Vinegar now too? 'So let me get this straight: you used *all* my bicarb and *all* my vinegar to create a frothy mess which lasted . . . how long? Minutes? Seconds? Anything else you needed for your "experiment"?' My smidge of sarcasm is lost on his seven-year-old self.

'No, nothing else. Well, a bit of washing-up liquid, that's all. And we didn't need *all* your vinegar, anyway – there's still a dribble left at the bottom of the bottle.' Disappointed at my not exactly ecstatic reaction to his chemical capers, his eyes lose a bit of their Pompeii sparkle.

'I'm sorry, Mum,' he mutters dejectedly, looking up at me, 'but it *was* an educational explosion!' His doe eyes touch my unscientific MOB heart.

'I'm sure it was,' I say putting an arm round his shoulders. 'It's just that you can't go using my ingredients to make a . . . a . . . mess without asking, without checking with me first – however educational that mess may be! And we can't make fairy cakes now, can we?' His face falls further. 'Tell you what,' I brighten, 'shall we make some shortbread instead?'

I may not always be able to understand the attraction of Etna, I may not yet have the key to my little boys' minds, but one thing I do know is that the way to their hearts is not so much through their heads as through their grumbling, always rumbling stomachs.

Personally, I have no recollection of ever pinching my mum's bicarb or vinegar as a small child. I canvas the opinions of my female friends; nope: none of them did either. Make-up maybe, to beautify our Girl's Worlds, face cream possibly, to slather on Sindy. But bicarb? Vinegar? No.

But when I mention the incident to the FOB later that night, his eyes light up like the now predictable Pompeii.

'Ah yes,' he recalls happily. I half expect him to add, 'I remember it well . . .', but he doesn't. 'I used to do all kinds of chemistry when I was a kid: homemade stink bombs, dancing raisins . . . We even did immiscible liquids once.'

I look at his animated face – blank. Think I must have been in H.E. cooking yet another crumble, while he was being a lad in the lab, doing scientific stuff.

'You know? Trying to mix oil and water together – only they don't.'

Nope, still not ringing any school bells for me.

'I'll never forget Mum being furious that I'd used all her olive oil . . .'

Now this is something I *can* understand. Not for the first time, I feel a certain empathetic understanding with my mother-in-law.

'Yes, but what about my bicarbonate of soda?' I try again.

'Maybe I'll see if the boys want to do it again tomorrow . . .' he says with a faraway look, usually reserved for building-project dreams. Apparently, he too has his sons' capacity for convenient hearing. 'The explosion's even better if you add glitter and glue!'

On the basis of this, my own extremely random research, I can now categorically claim that making a mess in the name of science is an important part of the mainly male mindset. That selfsame mindset which means that our family home, once a balanced amalgamation of husband and wife, has been almost totally transformed into an ode to the boy, a temple to testosterone, a monument to the machinations of the masculine mind.

For upstairs, our sons' bedroom walls – previously tastefully speckled with Paddington or Pooh – are now barely visible under a barrage of solar systems and full-scale maps. Lists of kings, queens and in-betweens reign supreme on the backs of doors, while 'Dangerous Doings for Boys' cover crannies and nooks.

It could be worse, I suppose.

Thus far, we appear to have escaped the unappetising prospect of having footballers or, God forbid, some topless totty, adorning their walls, but it's only, I feel sure, a matter of time. Before too long, I'll be confronted by Buffy as I put away their pants, come face to face with Ferdinand as I fumigate their duvets. Suddenly, up close and personal with Uranus doesn't seem quite so bad, after all.

Downstairs meanwhile, our beautiful bookshelves – once the eclectic preserve of novels and biographies – are now a boy rumble jumble of geometry and geology, mazes and maths. My eyes are subjected to finding Wally on an all-too-regular basis, what I don't know about every world record that ever was frankly ain't worth knowing and, until recently, I never knew (nor, I'm ashamed to admit, particularly cared) that the capital of Uzbekistan is ('Of *course*, Mum!') Tashkent. More and more, and often subconsciously, I find myself strangely drawn into a parallel universe where facts, and not the Fairy-populated Tales of my own female childhood, preside. Where information is everything and knowledge is king. And, however alien it may sometimes seem, this indecent exposure to the boy brain has done more for my grasp of geography than any amount of GCSE coursework ever could.

Thus, I am still amazed – but no longer fazed – by the constant barrage of boy questions and queries:

Exactly how many accidents have there been involving double-decker buses . . . ever?

How long does it take to get to Jamaica . . . on foot?

How *do* you give mouth-to-mouth resuscitation to a ladybird . . . and when can I try?

I may not always know the answers and, at times, frankly, my dears, I don't give a damn, but I understand it's important and know where to look.

Thus, I now know – after tens of hours of playing tedious Top Trumps – that while raptors are rubbish, it's T Rex who's best; that while Barosaurus is 'lame', he can't be beaten on height; and though Steggie is heavy, he's often outstripped on age.

And thus, somewhat scarily, I have even caught myself watching, and perchance appreciating, the historically unfathomable attractions of *Deadly 60*, *Dr Who* and (albeit infrequently) *Top Gear*. Like ivy, the male mentality is, it seems, wheedling its way in to my female-focused MOB mortar.

But it doesn't end there.

For if knowledge is king in our household of men, then gadgets and technology rank closer to God.

Turn on anything with a screen and my merely sporadically

hard-of-hearing sons become utterly deaf to my woman's world. Stupefied by Sonic, muted by Mario, my techno-boys plunge into a void populated only by Pokemons, by penguins and plot.

'Will you turn those things off and talk to each other!' I yell at my sofa of sons, each apparently engrossed in his own DS.

Sensible Son seems to reply without moving his lips. 'But we are, Mum. We're CO . . . MMUN . . . I . . . CATING!'

I'm at a loss to see how, given that if he or his brothers were interacting any less obviously, I'd be checking their pupils for the slightest signs of life. 'Look – we've joined up . . . we're sending each other messages.'

Partially mollified by the idea that maybe they are not, after all, living in an entirely 'solo' screen world, I lean over his shoulder. Are they debating the important differences between a town and a city? Discussing the advantages of iron over zinc? Assessing the impact of a famine or flood?

I squint myopically at the too-small text.

'"Stinky" has a kicking "k" in it, not a "curly" one,' I say. 'And I think you'll find that "bottom" is a more appropriate term.'

Just as I think I'm getting to grips with Planet Boy, I'm brought back to Oestrogen Earth – with a bump.

Aware that I still have a gap in truly understanding the mechanics of my offspring's minds, I adopt a more proactive approach to becoming fully lad-literate.

Stepping boldly away from the comfort zone of my house and the sink, I volunteer – yes, willingly put my name down – to accompany Sensible Son and his class on their next school trip. Not to the gender-neutral aquarium, nor even a female-friendly farm. No, this trip will take me to the underage equivalent of a

237

Beer Fest in Bremen: we are boarding the bus to the local science museum.

As we lurch to a halt outside the moonscape domes, my head is already throbbing with both the out-of-tune chanting from the back of the bus and the realisation that once inside, there can be no turning back. Once I walk into the domes, I will be entering a world that may *look* and *feel* familiar, which I may even be able to superficially explain, but about which my *actual* understanding, my *deep down* knowledge, remains – despite years of inhabiting it – decidedly limited. I am about to step into my own scientific abyss.

And so it is that I find myself, an hour or so later, sitting in an auditorium full of fresh – and not quite so fresh – faces, listening and watching, as the splendours of space are quite literally laid out before us. Craning my head towards the ceiling, I watch, spellbound, as stars sprinkle the sky, as constellations converge and as day turns to night to day again. Only mildly nauseous, thanks to the revolving screen and my propensity for vertigo, I am finally, *finally* shown, hear and – most critically – UNDERSTAND the fundamental facts that have remained outside my grasp for nigh on forty years.

'Eureka!' I only just refrain from shouting at the equally enthralled but, presumably, better-informed audience. Instead, I clasp Sensible Son's shoulder after the show.

'Wasn't that fantastic!' I gush, 'I learned so much . . . about the solar system, the constellations, how the sun goes round the earth, or . . . hang on . . . it's the other way round, isn't it? I can *never* remember!'

Shrugging my hand from his too-cool shoulder, he regards me with a disdain usually reserved for Binary Boy. 'The earth goes round the sun, of course. Come on, Mum, everyone knows that! It's *so* – like – obvious!'

I hasten to cover my ignorant tracks. 'Of course they do. I mean, I do . . . um . . . just checking! Right,' I say, 'just nipping to the loo!'

I scuttle to the Ladies, grab a pencil and paper from my bag and rapidly write my revelations down. Just in case I ever find I forget.

Later that evening, my head is still spinning from my solar school experience. The elation of my new-found knowledge is wearing off and, unlike my kids, it appears, I'm ready for bed. I look at the clock: 6.02 p.m. Good. The sun is most definitely over the yardarm as my GP Grandfather used to say, before pouring his darling wife a medicinal sherry. More importantly for *this* wife, however, is that any time after six means I can legitimately take off my clothes and slip into something more comfortable. Infinitely preferable to sherry any day.

I sneak into my bedroom to pull on my PJs. All seems to be remarkably quiet on the Western front – no screams, no 'Stop its', no 'It's not fairs' – so I creep into my sanctuary for a few furtive minutes.

My sanctuary is the sliver of our house which I call '*her*' home, where boys are banned and where the mistress is the MOB. My sanctuary is, since the arrival and delayed departure of builder Bob and his gang, my en suite.

Of course, attached as it is to the *master* bedroom, technically I share it with the FOB. Given, however, that thanks to his work he is more long-term lodger than permanent fixture, the en suite belongs, to all intents and purposes, to me.

So I have a stylish French film poster on the pristine white walls, there are candles (scented) dotted vacuously along the shelf and frivolous bottles of shower gel stand attractively to attention. The basin's spit-free, the loo seat stays down, the carpet is clean.

I love my en suite in an entirely disproportionate and unashamedly ridiculous fashion. I love it almost as much as I do my favourite morning mug, the one with the big blue and white flowers, the absence of which for my daily appointment with the *Today* team can cast my mood irrationally asunder.

Tit for tat, my band of merry men. There are some things about this Maid Marian you will *never* understand.

So, I'm looking in the mirror, basking in the inexplicable pleasure of my en suite space, and I realise that after a long day of sitting on buses and being about boys, my face is in desperate need of a clean. Reaching for my seldom-used bottle of cleansing fluid, I prepare for scrub-off.

'Who's pinched my cotton wool?' I roar, scrabbling about in the cabinet and emerging with an empty bag full only of air.

My biggest boy dares to enter the 'ladies-only' lair. 'Oh, er . . . sorry, Mum. We "borrowed" it last weekend to make Chinese lanterns with Dad . . . they were fantastic!' His blue eyes sparkle at this magical memory. 'You, er, you didn't need it, did you?'

I stare at his face, at once both astonishingly familiar, yet absolutely foreign . . . and suddenly I *see*.

I see that it doesn't actually matter that I don't 'get' the volcanic attractions of *my* baking bicarb or the pyromaniac potential of *my* cleansing cotton wool. That it's irrelevant that I sometimes struggle to share their 'me-first' mentality, that I can't always see the point of redistributing rocks. I understand that I can't, and probably shouldn't try to, get right inside and to grips with my little boys' brains. Because suddenly I see that it doesn't matter if the actions of my opposite-sex offspring aren't always logical and in tune with my MOB mind.

My sons are wired differently to me; so there. So what?

What matters, of course, is that the boys live happily, healthily, free to be 'hes', while I trundle alongside them in our boy-dominated domain, free to *think* and *feel* (if not always *be*) 'she'.

Mother Earth orbiting – in celestial harmony – around her Son.

I realise too that I will never need to commit the concept to paper, ever again.

'No, I didn't need it really,' I say, kissing his thoughtful, but oh-*so* boy, brow.

I put the empty bag in the bin, and use loo roll instead.

How to remember the order of the planets:
A MOB's Manic Monday-morning Mnemonic

Mum's	**M**ercury
Very	**V**enus
Easily	**E**arth
Mad	**M**ars
Just	**J**upiter
Say	**S**aturn
U	**U**ranus
Need	**N**eptune
Packed-lunch	**P**luto

. . . although by the time you can commit this mnemonic to memory, your smart-alec son will inform you that Pluto may well no longer actually be a planet. I'd throw in the tea towel now, if I were you.

You understand the male mindset when . . .

- You instinctively know the difference between a front loader and a JCB. You may even care.
- What you don't know about the offside rule/the prowess of performance cars/the average speed of a slug (delete as applicable), frankly, ain't worth knowing.
- You are still pointing out tractors/fire engines/ double-decker buses long after they've ceased to be of any interest to your sons.
- You are pointing out all of the above when you are driving alone.
- You've sat through (and enjoyed) *Star Trek* more times than *Spooks*.
- You can identify a Ferrari on the road and know that it's cool.
- You understand why your 'It's bedtime' and their 'But . . . it's live football!' aren't entirely compatible.
- You give equal weight and attention to questions about where that 'minuscule triangular see-through piece of yellow Lego that I was using last week when I was building a helicopter' is . . . and about when the world will end.
- You realise that the sooner you perfect that 'I'm-intrigued-and-listening' look, the easier it will be to get on with making tea.
- You can correct your son when he plants a sloppy kiss on your lips and informs you that the longest kiss ever lasted sixteen and a quarter days. Because I think that you'll find it was sixteen and a half.

How to make your own Vinegar Volcano

You will need:

- Your mother's bottle of vinegar she's been keeping for chutney
- Your mother's bicarbonate of soda she's been saving for cakes
- Food colouring (to make your demonstration more dramatic and it's great for staining clothes)
- A jar (again, possibly the nice one she's been keeping for the condiments)
- The entirety of the kitchen table and most of the floor
- Glitter (optional)

Step 1: Do not cover the table with newspaper or yourselves with an apron.

Step 2: Place 2 tablespoons of baking soda in the jar. Spill the rest on the floor – what does it matter . . . it's only white powder.

Step 3: Add a few drops (oh, go on then, the entire bottle) of food colouring to ¼ cup of warm water.

Step 4: Add the water and colouring to the baking soda. Ensure that as much as possible drips on to the table.

Step 5: Add ½ cup of vinegar (and a bit more for good measure) to the mixture.

Step 6: Peer closely into the jar – NO DON'T – that was an unfunny joke!

Step 7: Stand well back and watch, in amazement and awe, as Mount Etna erupts all over the floor.

Step 8: Once the eruption is over, lose interest immediately. Leave the lava spill for later, and turn on the TV.

They may not always want to marry their mum

I'm on the landing outside the bathroom door, attempting to fold and house yet another wash basket full of shirts, shorts and miscellaneous socks. I examine a predictably dark item of clothing: is this one of Sensible Son's sloppy shirts or have I put one of my own tighter tops in a too-hot wash? I check the label and realise, despondently, that the latter is the case. Oh dear, I think, chucking it towards the top of stairs – another one for the second-hand clothing store. While Posh Spice may get away with skintight after the births of *her* boys, this mere-mortal MOB, unfortunately, cannot.

With half my mind on Victoria's virtues and half an ear on my boys in the bath, I poke my head around the door and listen in on their random ramblings.

'Who's your best friend at school?' Binary Boy asks Feisty Fellow.

'I have gamillions,' says his reception-going brother, removing his hands from the water and preparing to count. He runs out of fingers and gives up. 'More 'n ten, anyhows.'

'Those are your *boy* friends,' points out the more socially savvy Binary Boy. 'Who are your *girl* friends?' He's now in Year 2 and therefore an expert on PHSE and all aspects emotional.

Feisty Fellow stares into space, and considers for a moment. 'Well, I did have two . . . but now it's only Katie that I'm gonna marry. I fink I dumped Sarah. Hang on . . . was it Sarah? Yeah, I dumped Sarah yesterday!'

His brother receives this news with a wise, unsurprised nod. 'Hmmm, probably easier with just the one, anyway.'

'That's what I fought,' says his smaller sibling, happily. Conversation apparently closed, they pick up their Action Men and resume their bath battle.

I stop, mid-sock stuffing, both amused and aghast. The idea of my barely-out-of-rusks boys discussing girlfriends at all is bad enough, but '*dumped*'? Where on earth have my babies picked up this teenage terminology? Do they have any idea what they are talking about? And hey, wait a minute – Feisty Fellow has always maintained that he's going to marry ME, not some floozy four-year-old he's only just met! Surely I, his mother, am the most important, the most 'bootiful' lady in his life . . . in all their lives. Aren't I?

I resume my sock stuffing with renewed vigour, recognising – if not at all relishing – the possibility that at some point in the hopefully *very* distant future, I may be forced to relinquish my role as Number-One Woman to my squadron of sons. And, as the only Queen in this Castle of Kings, this is not a happy thought.

A few weeks after the bath-time banter, Gorgeous Girl comes for a sleepover with Sensible Son.

Despite the fact that our house is teeming with testosterone, it appears that our boys are extremely popular with their female friends. And, as a multiple MOB who could well have been destined for an after-school life of *only* khaki and cars, this is a constant source of pleasure and pride.

Since the boys were small, the FOB and I have worked hard to encourage our children to play with anyone and everyone, regardless of their bodily bulges, or indeed the colour of their Crocs. Inevitably perhaps, as they get older and are more influenced by outside expectations and internal realisations, they have begun to gravitate away from the girls, towards the more bawdy of boys. However, the process of sexual streamlining seems to be gratifyingly gradual, and so it is that Sensible Son is often one of a smattering of boys at female friends' parties, Binary Boy flits effortlessly between the sugar and slug sexes and (despite the tales of his most recently ruptured relationship) even Feisty Fellow is tickled pink by the attentions of the gaggles of girls who 'mummy' him in the playground to within an inch of his life.

So, instead of an all-boy bedtime, on this occasion, it is a Gorgeous Girl who comes to stay.

She arrives, and I accompany her and her Cath Kidston case upstairs.

I show her into our eldest boy's room. Sensible Son (suddenly not *quite* so sensible) bounds on to his bed. Gorgeous Girl twirls on her toes, clutches her teddy and stands, suddenly shy and obviously unsure of quite what to do next.

'D'ya like my map?' asks Sensible Son proudly, indicating the chart which covers almost the entirety of his wall.

She nods, chews her lip and continues her stationary twirl.

'D'ya like my Techno Ball battery-powered marble run?' he asks again, flicking the 'On' switch to demonstrate its apparently captivating capabilities.

She nods and smiles, but stays rooted to the spot.

Running out of fascinating features and ever eager to please, he gestures towards his bookcase. 'D'ya like my books?' he pleads enthusiastically. 'Look . . . I've got all the *Horrid Henry* . . .' – he registers her lack of interest – '*Swallows and Amazons*? *Famous Five*?' She grins and kneels down beside him, picking up one of his well-thumbed editions. Their heads bow towards each other as they find their common ground . . . and I leave them to it.

Later that evening, Gorgeous Girl has, it appears, well and truly bonded with my slightly scary trio.

249

She trumps at the table, she burps like the best of them, and (markedly more slowly) she finishes her food. Squished on to one sofa between Binary Boy and Sensible Son with Feisty Fellow on her lap, and with the FOB and I sitting safely on the other side of the room, she giggles gleefully at *Ice Age* antics, the slapstick humour crossing all potential gaps between generations and gender. And when it's time for bed, she protests like the rest, insisting on a sky ride on the FOB's thankfully strong shoulders, before stripping off to wash, with uninhibited abandon.

After a busy-boy day, my muck magnets and their girl guest are back in the bath.

Somehow, they manage to squeeze all four too-big bodies into our horizontally challenged bath without (maybe Archimedes was wrong after all?) totally emptying the tub. One by one, they wash, play and splash, waiting to step obligingly out to be dried.

'This fourth child business is a doddle,' I think smugly, fluffy towel in hand, 'and it *is* fun to have some female company for a change.' In this moment of misplaced optimism, the barking, and at times highly irritating, idea of 'going for a girl' doesn't seem *quite* so ridiculous after all . . .

I turn to pitch my impulsive plan to the FOB, when a sudden screech brings me back to he-ality with a bump.

Feisty Fellow is kicking off.

Instead of slipping on his pyjamas and sloping off for a story as he usually does, the tantalising presence of Gorgeous Girl brings out in him an almost primeval predilection for showing off. Casting his towel aside, he leaps into the air, hollering and howling. Legs akimbo, he wiggles his bottom in the direction of our guest's fascinated but somewhat perplexed face, like an overenthusiastic male baboon. He lets out an inadvertent fart; all hell breaks loose.

Binary Boy jumps out of the bath, soaking first the mat and then his mother as he canters uncontrollably into the fray. A gangly colt, he snorts and cavorts, all arms and overly lanky limbs. Gorgeous Girl watches his display in stunned silence. Shaking his mock mane, he lets out a high-pitched whinny, before, thankfully, galloping off into the night.

Sensing that this is his moment, Sensible Son adopts an altogether more subtle approach to attracting Gorgeous Girl's already divided attention. Rising from the water, he dries himself casually off, before modestly modelling his long-john pyjamas. Puffing and preening with the prowess of a peacock, he takes the now ready-for-bed Gorgeous Girl by the hand and leads her to his room. 'She's sleeping in here . . . with me!' he announces and slams the door emphatically shut.

His brothers stop mid-gallop, mid-wiggle. Age over beauty, they unwittingly accept and hurtle, beaten, back to their beds.

The moment of male madness is apparently over and the FOB and I divide and conquer to read to our vanquished suitors, leaving Sensible Son and Gorgeous Girl to the enduring attractions of Julian and George. Mercifully, it appears that Morpurgo and Mr Men mend even the most broken of hearts.

So it is that this completely innocuous initiation into the world of future flirtations gives me a taste – albeit merely a morsel – of things to come. In my mind, I flash forward to a time when my strapping sons will tower over their mini-MOB, when the house will be full of aftershave and Adam's apples, when the boys will compete (this goes without saying) for the most gorgeous, gregarious of girls, huffing and puffing around each other like over-inflated penguins. To a time when I will look in the mirror and realise that, even through their love-blind, baby-biased eyes, I am no longer the fairest of them *all*.

And thus I start (I said, *start*) to concede that one day

– possibly, probably, even, OK, hopefully – this Matriarch MOB will be replaced, first by grungy girlfriends and then by The One. That one day they will meet and marry their very own Snow Whites.

In line with my long-standing 'note to self' to tackle any sexual pigeonholing, I embark on a programme of domestication with my increasingly accomplished, if not always enthusiastic, hubbies-to-be. For whichever Snow Whites eventually win the battle for my beloved boys' hearts, they will not be disappointed on the domestic front. My Princely progeny will not only be Charming, but also competent in the kitchen, able to iron, willing to wash.

I begin by asking them what the FOB does about the house, hoping to highlight the already revolutionised role of the modern man.

'He changes the light bulbs,' says Sensible Son.

'He charges the batteries,' adds Binary Boy.

'He fixes things . . . and when you're not here he does make *awesum* banoffee pie!' throws in Feisty Fellow. Er, hello . . . First 'dumped', now 'awesome'. And hang on, it's that banoffee pie again . . . how does that fit in with my five-a-day philosophy? One banana per pie does not a portion make.

Fortunately, that discussion will, unlike this more pressing one and unlike the presumably swiftly scoffed pud, have to keep.

'Yes . . . but what does he do on a regular basis? The cleaning? The cooking?' I prompt in a bid to pinpoint at least some understanding of their (to my mind, anyway) not undomesticated dad. While my Forces-bred spouse doesn't often brandish a bog brush, his creases are legendary, his sewing is skilled and he knows where the Hoover is kept, and is even capable of switching it on. Emptying the bag is, understandably, beyond him . . . but that's another story.

252

'So what *does* Dad do at home, boys . . . to help?'

Three faces – each bearing hallmarks of their revered but around-the-house apparently unemployed father – stare back at me. Blank.

We work hard to address this perceived domestic imbalance.

Swiftly and sharply, I make it clear to my boys big *and* small, that I am neither enamoured with, nor responsible for, the picking up of pants.

'What'sh I put in the dishwasher?' asks my well-conditioned, if verbally confused youngest son, brandishing his adventure-grimy garb. Thanks to non-stop nagging, my boys now know what a wash basket's for and have even been seen to – get this – *automatically* lift the lid and put their clothes *inside,* rather than leaving them hopefully on top for the Female Wash Fairy. Nothing short of a major miracle for a bloke of any age, moan fellow MOG and MOB friends alike. While the gender of our offspring may differ, that of our intermittently ineffective other halves does not.

From day 'tot', I encourage independence (as well as maxi-mising kip) by letting them put their own breakfasts into bowls.

'Can you get my Noddy spoon out for me please?' I hear Feisty Fellow ask his taller brother through our too-thin floor-boards. I roll over in bed and prepare to enjoy a few more seconds of slumber. 'Can you get me my Ben 10 cup?' I hear him ask his still surprisingly helpful sibling. I smile sleepily at this uncommon exhibition of brotherly bonding, and smother a yawn. 'Can you make me some porridge?'

Grabbing my dressing gown, I yelp out of bed and stumble down the stairs. Too late to stem a milk slick the size of Lake Titicaca, too late to stop the snow storm of oats. But it's worth it, I remind myself, grabbing a brush in one hand, the cloth in the other: I'm investing in Snow White's, and indeed my own, forthcoming freedom.

And as soon as they can read (and even before), the boys are exposed to Nigella, Delia and Hugh.

'Who wants to help make muffins?' I shout at my sons. I try again. 'OK, who wants to make *chocolate* muffins?'

A jumble of Jamies run for a stool and we embark on lessons in far-from-lean cuisine. So what if they eat more of the mixture than they slop in the cases? So what if each cake contains more bogeys than flour? So what if my crafty courgette creations must be smothered in chocolate? So what? If cooking with cocoa steers my boys towards Blumenthal, then even I can accept the odd surfeit of sweet.

And so it is that entirely oblivious to my maternal motivations, the boys continue their home economics education, ingesting a curriculum that will take them from hopeless homme to highly capable catch. As they progress from stage one to stove two, I am beginning to almost envy the currently faceless, but (probably) future (Mrs) Snow Whites.

Not only, I realise, because these lucky ladies will be the direct beneficiaries of their culinary talents, their home-grown expertise, their domestic prowess. No, not only because of that. I'm beginning to envy them because it also occurs to me that my envisaged daughters-in-law, my fictional Snow Whites, will be holding more than merely the hands and the hearts of my beloved boys. The more I think about it, the more I am aware that in my fictitious future, it will be the Snow White wives and not Wicked Mother-me who will, by then, be completely 'in charge'. In charge of *my* sons, in charge of *their* offspring, of when, where and how much *I* get to figure in *their* family life. I realise with foreboding that in the Fairy Tale of this future, they, and not me, will be holding all the cards.

I share this not-altogether-rocking revelation at our monthly meeting of multiple MOB minds.

'Oooh yes,' salivates Extreme MOB, picking up on – but apparently missing – my painful point, 'you're absolutely right about being in charge. It's great being a daughter-in-law . . . especially now we have kids! As *his* wife and *their* mother, you wield all the power over *their* son, *their* grandchildren . . . *them*.' She pauses, licks her lips, takes another sip of blood-red wine, 'And the in-laws know it!'

I stare at her, shocked by the somewhat warped delight she appears to be taking from her prime position as Wife of the Son. I put my original point to her again, more bluntly this time.

'The problem is, Extreme MOB, won't you – like me – be walking in your *mother*-in-law's shoes at some point in the future? Won't we, as the mothers of the husbands and not of their wives, always be in some ways that "Other Woman"? Always be the mother-*in-law* of the wife, never be the actual mother of The Mum . . .' She gawps at me, trying to extract the sense of what I am saying through the words and the wine. 'As multiple MOBs, we will never be the number-one Granny . . . always be stuck as secondary – not senior – Gran.'

The room is struck silent as we take on board the undoubted implications of what has become a shared MOB moment.

We reflect on our own maternal experiences.

However strong the bond with our mothers-in-law, however wonderful the mothers of our husbands are, most of us (though admittedly not all) had *our* mums around at the births and call *our* mums when times are tough. We are the daughters, the wives, the mothers – and we call the shots. And, on the whole, we ask *our* mums, not his.

And now, as only MOBs, and not MOGs, we will quietly wait to be summonsed by our son's wife, the mother of his children, the accepted social networker, rather than expecting a call from our own, more than likely, phone-phobic son. As mothers-in-law, as paternal grandparents, we may be liked, we may be loved, we may even (like my own boys' paternal GOBs) be adored. But when push comes to inevitable shove, we will always accede to the wishes and wants of our daughters-in-law and take second place to the number-one Gran.

We murmur our less-than-ecstatic agreement with this academically supported suggestion.

I try to lighten the tone. 'Anyway, that's what Queen Victoria said, apparently. And Hugh Fearnley-Whittingstall's mum. So,' I look at the sea of forlorn MOB masks, 'it must be true!'

Ah, Hugh Fearnley-Whittingstall . . . now, there is a man who'd make any MOB proud. Thankfully, the discussion turns from deep and meaningful towards seaweed and sausages, and our light-hearted nocturnal nattering resumes.

The discussion may be over, but I bear my future secondary status very much in mind as I precociously rehearse my planned progress from Mother of Boy to In-law of Girl. I may never be the Mother of the Bride, may never be the number-one Nan, but, with perseverance, patience and practice, I can easily be that bit on Snow White's side.

I can, I decide, choose to see my sons' spouses as female friends, rather than fatal foe; as welcome companions, not emotional competition; as a happy and healthy part of my boys' inescapable transition from tied to my apron strings to tying their own knot.

I can weep at their weddings . . . but then I will stop.

For I will be gaining a daughter – not losing a son. For – if they are able and want to – they will have children and I will become a Grandmother and I will offer my, albeit secondary, services as nocturnal nanny and daytime doula. For I will finally, finally have someone around who can cry at *Casualty*, who compliments my hair, who may even enjoy the odd saunter round shops.

A Princess who, like me, loves my boys, but who also likes me.

Some time later, I sit on the edge of Feisty Fellow's bed, stroking his hair to sleep. As the world unwinds, and in the absence of sleepovers (however gorgeous the girl undoubtedly is), this is one of my favourite times of the day.

'I love you, Mummy . . .' he murmurs, drowsily.

'I love you too . . . thiiiiss much!' I spread my arms wide in strict accordance with our night-time regime.

'I will always love you, Mummy . . . even when yous not my mummy any more, even when I's married to my own mummy!'

'You mean "wife" . . . your own wife. And anyway, even if you get married, even when you're a grown-up, I'll still be your mummy,' I say, reassuring both him and my own still (can't help it) selfish self.

He looks at me incredulously. 'Even when I'm really old . . . as old as you?'

I nod; laugh. 'Even then!'

He ponders, then sighs.

'Anyway, I'm not marrying Katie any more. She dumped me. Today. She's gonna marry Sam 'stead.' My over-attached heart plummets for my ditched darling. I slip my hand in his, squeeze it hard and savour the moment, knowing that Snow White is still stuck in the forest of the future.

And the Queen crown is mine for a little while longer.

257

A by-no-means exhaustive list of my Manuals of Motherhood

- *Raising Boys* (Steve Biddulph)
- *The New Contented Little Baby Book* (Gina Ford)
- *Men are from Mars, Women are from Venus* (John Gray)
- *New Toddler Taming* (Dr Christopher Green)
- *Beyond Toddlerdom* (Dr Christopher Green)
- *Child of Our Time* (Tessa Livingstone)
- *Siblings Without Rivalry* (Adele Faber & Elaine Mazlish)
- *Why Men Don't Listen & Women Can't Read Maps* (Allan & Barbara Pease)
- *Your Baby & Child: From Birth to Age Five* (Penelope Leach)

> '*A son is a son till he takes him a wife, a daughter is a daughter all of her life*' *(Irish saying)*
> Discuss this with fellow MOBs, with tissues and wine.

> '*A man loves his sweetheart the most, his wife the best, but his mother the longest*' *(another Irish saying)*
> Don't bother to discuss.
> Just print this out and stick on the front of the fridge.

PS . . .

I finished reading a book last week. Not just *Horrid Henry* or *Thomas the Tank Engine*. No, a real-life, proper grown-up book without pictures and everything. A momentous occasion in every MOB's life.

I celebrated with a cup of scalding hot coffee. I drank it on the sofa, looking out at the lawn. No one jumped, bumped or leaped on to or over me. I just sat and sipped and thought, in silence.

Then, coffee break over, I vacuumed the house. All of it. No one rode the Dyson as if it were Red Rum. No one pulled out the plug or switched off the socket. No one whinged and whined at me until they could 'elp. I just got it quickly and quietly done.

And it made me think. What else can I do now that I couldn't before? How is my life different nowadays from way back then? Is there no end to the possibilities for this post-manic-days MOB?

For avocado and banana are but a distant-mush memory and scaffolding and soft play mere ghosts of the past. The leftover nappy sacks can go to the dogs.

The conversations at the dinner table are surprisingly sophisticated, even actually entertaining. True, the farting's still funny and boy, can they burp, but at least now the jokes about bottoms are mainly outside, and often in French. And 'caca' is somehow far preferable to poo.

As the boys morph frighteningly fast from boy towards man,

the levels of chaos and general confusion are on the decline. The food bills, unfortunately, are not.

Fridge almost empty, I head back to the supermarket. It's a Saturday, so unusually for the modern me, I'm not shopping alone.

Sensible Son ('Let me push it, Mum, I'm stronger than you!') takes charge of the trolley.

Binary Boy ('Are you sure it's 300 *grams* and not *kilos* of ham we want?') looks after, looks at and ticks off the list.

Feisty Fellow ('Can you time me, Daddy, while I go get the grapes?') revels in his role as chief fetcher of food.

So the FOB and I stand back and watch as our boys take control. Occasionally, I am brought in to arbitrate on the choice of sweet treats or the FOB reaches high for yet another box of own-brand cereal. I fear it won't be long before even these roles are redundant.

A tap on the shoulder brings me back from basics with a bump. I turn to face the aggressor, fearfully wondering what I've done wrong today. Has Sensible Son blundered into some poor shopper's shins? Has Binary Boy inadvertently pinched another purchaser's produce? Has Feisty Fellow been over-fingering the fruit?

'I just wanted to tell you what gorgeous children you have . . .' says a Mrs Pepperpot-type person, gesturing towards our, admittedly, on this occasion, angelic-looking sons, 'and so well-behaved!'

'Well . . . er . . . thank you,' I say, beaming, first at her, and then at my boys. She turns and prepares to shuffle to the sprouts.

'Two boys and a girl,' she mutters to no one in particular. 'How lovely . . . how perfect!'

I open my mouth, automatically, to correct her. To tell her that there is no girl. To inform her that instead I have been blessed with 'just boys'. And then I stop. I smile.

262

'Perfect? Aren't they just!' I say. 'Just perfect.'

Sensible Son wriggles and jiggles and bounces on the spot. 'I need to go to the toilet, Mum.'

'Oh, er . . . same here, same here,' Binary Boy pipes up predictably. 'Where are the loos?'

Feisty Fellow, never one to be left behind, adds his voice to the throng. 'Me too, Mummy, me too. I need a weeeee!'

I look despairingly at my still incapable-of-waiting testosterone troop. 'Why didn't you go before we came out? Didn't you hear me when I said that you should?'

A united band of brothers, they shake their heads.

'Come on then,' I grumble, taking the trolley and turning around, 'the loos are back over this way.'

We arrive at the lavatories. The FOB heads for the Gents, Sensible Son and Binary Boy follow in their father's footsteps. Feisty Fellow, however, hangs on to my hand.

'Oh no you don't, young man!' I push him gently in the direction of the male toilets – 'I think it's about time you started going with your dad!' – and head instead for the luxury of the Ladies.

To pee, seat down, alone and in peace.

Just one of the benefits of belonging to the MOB.

Acknowledgements

They say you should never judge a book by its cover. And of course, like so many others, I did. But the production and publication of *MOB Rule* has changed all that. It has opened my eyes to quite how many people are involved in publishing each and every book.

As I am frequently reminded, I have a tendency to talk so here I will do my very best to be brief.

To my family and friends who have lived, breathed and sometimes even experienced *MOB Rule*: thank you for your enthusiasm, patience, coffees and chat.

To Neil Taylor, my agent, friend and boys' football coach: thank you for putting your time and faith into an unknown author.

To the highly professional yet totally personal team at Bloomsbury: thank you all for transforming my 'words on a page' into a 'real-life' book. And to my editor in particular, Helen Garnons-Williams: thank you for your ever-so-light touch with astonishing effect.

To my husband, FOB and best friend, Charles: thank you for always believing in me, even when I don't!

And finally, to my boys: thank you Toby, Barney and Josh, for being inspiring, adorable, but most importantly, you.

A NOTE ON THE AUTHOR

Hannah Evans has previously explored the world of the MOB in a number of articles, most notably in the *Guardian*. She lives with her husband and three boys in Devon.

The text of this book is set in Bembo. This type was first used in 1495 by the Venetian printer Aldus Manutius for Cardinal Bembo's *De Aetna*, and was cut for Manutius by Francesco Griffo. It was one of the types used by Claude Garamond (1480–1561) as a model for his Romain de L'Université, and so it was the forerunner of what became standard European type for the following two centuries. Its modern form follows the original types and was designed for Monotype in 1929.